HERE I STAND

The Faith of a Radical

JOHN J. VINCENT

LONDON
EPWORTH PRESS

FIRST PUBLISHED IN 1967
BY EPWORTH PRESS
(Book Steward: Frank H. Cumbers)

Printed in Great Britain
by Page & Thomas Limited
Chesham, Buckinghamshire

To

LORD SOPER

Peer of Methodist Radicals

The author expresses his thanks to the editors for their permission to include material which first appeared in their journals; to the Rev. Albert van den Heuvel for his ready agreement to the utilization of his Coventry address for chapter 9; and to the Rev. Gordon Wakefield, to whose project for a *Christ and Methodism Debate* symposium this must be the sole memorial, but whose help and co-operation in assembling this volume have been a great encouragement.

Contents

Foreword

> In a few years, I am sure we shall all smile about what is said (and sometimes shouted) in the following pages. History moves quickly, and we change within it. We all now need to start building again. The movement of protest is old enough to start the work of reconstruction.

So Albert van den Heuvel in his Foreword to *The Humiliation of the Church*. I agree, and the words can serve as text for my little book. If we are writing for all posterity, we shall not know. We simply have to say what is given us to say. And shout it. For the Church, and we ourselves, learn so slowly.

All serious Christian thinking and action is also self-confession. Hence, what we shout is always 'where we stand'. If anyone still feels it impertinent that I took the title, *Here I Stand*, I can but say that I was invited to do so.

The purpose of the booklet is twofold. First, to set out the lines of 'Christocentric Radicalism', and to show how this position is both necessitated by the unsatisfactory nature of other positions, and also pregnant with new possibilities for a radicalism which is genuinely Christian as well as thoroughly world-affirming. Here I have stated simply what I have developed in greater detail in other work.

The second purpose is simply to give the many who ask for it a handy summary of what I have been saying and writing recently, not least since so many find it new, difficult, objectionable or the only hope!

JOHN J. VINCENT

Champness Hall, Rochdale
August 1967

Part I. Here I Stand*

*An expanded form of the Lecture given at the 400th Anniversary Celebrations of the Welsh New Testament, Aberystwyth, 26 July 1967

1 Rumblings of a New Reformation

THERE are some texts which few preachers are brash enough to try to preach on; and some moments of history which few men would ever claim to emulate. Such a moment, perhaps, was when Martin Luther, on the 17th of April 1521, stood before his spiritual and material peers at the Diet of Worms, embarrassed, fearful and gauche, amazed that the glaring truth to him so clear was still concealed to others:

> My conscience is captive to the word of God. I cannot and I will not recant anything. To go against conscience is neither right nor safe. Here I stand. I can do no other. May God help me. Amen.

Whether he actually said, *Hier stehe ich: ich kann nicht anders* is historically disputable. But that is merely to say that if Luther did not say it, he was certainly entitled to.

One is therefore unlikely to choose this title, 'Here I Stand', and is only emboldened to accept it when offered because to fail to do so would be to fail to stand by the truth as one sees it, or is given to see it. And if the previous night, a conservative-evangelical (John R. W. Stott) did not fear to speak on the theme, then certainly a radical should not. The 'liberal' position, on which I refused to speak, thus remains unstated, except that I shall differentiate my position from that of the liberal as well as from that of the conservative-evangelical.

Implicit in this is the claim that there is a position clearly enough defined in the contemporary theological spectrum to be called 'radical'. I believe that there is, although it will become plain that I do not side with many who today call themselves radicals. Thus, Bishop John Robinson described a book of mine which criticized with almost equal enthusiasm the evangelical and the liberal-radical positions as 'Rocking the radical boat, too'.

This, at any rate, is our present situation: one in which whatever was true from the past has to be discovered, fought for and defined all over again; one in which we live by a few truths firmly held rather than by massive systems laboriously constructed; one in which all the old positions have shifted, and many are left floundering. I believe there is a truly radical position, although it is only just emerging; and I do not believe that there is simply a 'radical wing' on the old positions, which would be something much less than what I now see emerging. The uncertainties of our present situation, in my judgement, are the Erasmian humanism which precedes the true Reformation. But I also think that they are entitled to be regarded as the forerunners of a true Christian radicalism.

In his recent book, *The Old Reformation and the New*, Dr Gordon Rupp has delineated three ingredients in the first Reformation: Crisis of the Word; Crisis of Communication; and Crisis of Compassion. We have not yet got a New Reformation; there may never be one. But these three elements I would certainly claim belong to any true Christian radicalism.

First, a true Christian radicalism derives from sone new element in the Word. I stand with the Independent, John Robinson, in believing that God has more truth and light yet to break forth of his 'holy Word'. The first Reformation started with just such an impetus. As Luther said, 'The Word did it all. I left it to the Word.' But it was, of course, a new part of the Word which gave the Reformation its distinctive theology – the part of the Word which we call 'justification by faith', the principle of *sola fide*. I take my stand on the Word. But, like the first Reformers, I believe that there is some *particular* Word, some hitherto hidden Word, some Word which is 'forked lightning' for this moment, some Word of the Living Christ now.

Second, a true Christian radicalism derives from and precipitates a crisis of Communication. Bible translation, exposition, teaching and debate egg on the crisis of the Word, and are created anew out of it. One result of the first Reformation in this area was the translation and publication of the Welsh New Testament in 1567 which we commemorate this week. Today we have our plethora of new translations. But the crisis of new exposition which will make all our theology books out of date, the crisis of teaching method which will get us out of our pulpits into new life-related encounter of the Living Word with living man, the crisis of word and action within the institutional Church which will come from a new recognition of the nature of the Church – these things (let alone factors like television, the disappearance of the seven-day cycle, and the speed of technological progress) will produce a radical Church which few today would recognize, save that it will still contain, live by, and embody the mysteries of Jesus.

What the mysteries of Jesus are all about is the essential ingredient of the third element, the crisis in Compassion. Here I would insist that the new Reformation for our times will only come within the Church when it is forced to reckon with a 'new form of Christ in the world'. The twentieth-century Christian style of life for which we seek will take the form of the servant not because we can outdo the good humanists but because Jesus, having the secular form of the invisible God, took the form of a Servant. What this means, the Christian radical will learn often equally from the lines of Christ's own ministries and from the needs of contemporary man and society. Christian faith consists in presuming to say that the two, at least at crucial times, coincide. If the emerging radical Church seems at times pragmatic and materialistic, it is because –

at least for my money – it seeks to discover and work with the dynamics of Christ already working in the world.

This lecture, of course, is mainly concerned with the 'crisis of the Word'. Yet I would insist that the absence of wide experiment and risk-taking in Communication, and the absence of deep theological-political thinking and action in Compassion, in many cases obscures the desperate necessity, even in terms of the Church as it is and the world as it is, of radical theological rethinking.

As for that radical theological rethinking, all that I can attempt in this space is to name areas and slogans, indicating here and there how where I stand relates to other positions, especially the evangelical and the liberal.

I shall call my position 'Christocentric Radicalism', in order to distinguish it, on the one hand, from the Anglican liberal-radicalism of John Robinson and others, and, on the other hand, from the Christian-atheism radicalism of the American 'Death of God' theologians (Thomas Altizer, William Hamilton, etc.). At present, there is a great deal of ferment in theology, and this is not the time or place to sort out the enormous variety of views within the radical camp. In one sense, we are all more or less glad to be tarred with the same brush, as the orientation of our work, and the practical outcome of it, often lead us to the same places. This is equally true of two Roman Catholic groups: the Marxist-Catholic writers of *The New Left Church*, and the Dutch progressives. Whatever divides us, a common feeling unites us: that we must be *honest*, honest about the piece of ground given us to stand on, honest about where we differ from the past, honest about where we see things must move in the future. None of us, thank God, knows it all. We all proceed, in fear and trembling, in the shadow of Karl Barth's four prerequisites for the theologians: wonder, concern, commitment, and faith. We all confess that, often, we have to speak as fools. But we all confess that we cannot do other than speak.

2 The search for a Contemporary Gospel

I THINK that the point at which the radical takes his departure from the non-radical is simply on the basic meaning of the Gospel. There is a vast and impressive consensus, which reconciles conservative-evangelicals and Roman Catholics, Bultmannites and Southern Baptists, Liberals and Lutherans, that the Christian Gospel is that Christ died for our sins and was raised for our justification.

In other words, the Gospel is the Pauline Gospel, which can be read into Acts, and into Mark. One 'believes' when one is prepared to say: 'Christ died for me.' One becomes a Christian when one is 'converted' to this understanding of God and man. One is 'saved' by one's 'faith' in the atoning death, and one lives by the forgiveness and grace thus released, in the expectation of a personal heaven hereafter.

This understanding of Christianity has inspired a great and constantly renewed tradition, particularly in the West. It can be illustrated from the hymns of the Middle Ages or from those of Luther, Wesley or Sankey and Moody. It dictates alike the theology of the Roman Mass, the Reformation Confessions, the Gospel choruses, the Anglican Prayer Book. And it is this understanding of Christianity which seems to the radical to be basically impossible and inadequate – ridiculous, not in Paul's sense of the cross as a *skandalon*, but ridiculous in the sense that it is not borne out by the facts of the Gospels or the facts of personal experience.

Recently, at the Conference of the Renewal Group, fourteen of us sat in a Commission entitled, 'What is the

Gospel?' After three hours of sessions, we decided to set down what the Gospel was for each one of us. We took ten minutes of silence, and each wrote his own 'confession'. The result was deeply revealing.

The Gospel is that the universe is law-like; that this is discoverable; and that Jesus is a symbol and guarantee of both.

The Gospel is that my interpretations of the New Testament cartoons of Jesus correspond to basic realities of existence; notably, that Jesus, the man for others, is vindicated, and that the reality vindicating Jesus has faith in me.

The Gospel is about the *well-being* of the universe; that ultimate ruin is a lie.

The Gospel is the discovery of the significance of Jesus, the reasons for it and the consequences of it.

The Gospel is that there are values and meanings in life which I can and do become increasingly aware of; and I find Jesus the ground, key and validator of this.

The Gospel is that God loves the world he made and is bringing it back to perfection through Christ.

The Gospel is the announcement of man's freedom, and the claim that he is now to be *treated* as free. Disease, economic injustice and death are to be removed as they hinder this; faith, hope, love, etc. are to be prized as they make for man's freedom.

The Gospel is that the Spirit of the Lord is upon Jesus, for he has anointed him, and sent him to proclaim good news to the poor, release to the captives, and sight for the blind, and proclaim a time in which man can find favour with God.

The Gospel is that fascination with Jesus as a person leads to commitment that this is the way things should be; and that I find myself integrated around Jesus, bringing peace, purpose and meaning. Christ is not the bearer of the good news; he *is* the good news.

The Gospel is all the wonderful and terrifying things like compassion, love, obedience, forgiveness, sacrifice, which the Christian Church and faith (and I) struggle with because of the impact of Jesus.

The Gospel is that all creation, including all my life past and present, is utterly received, approved and pronounced good by God, and that this lays a claim on me to affirm my life and all that exists, and offers me a new possibility to live as the significant event in history that I am.

The Gospel is the life and sayings of Jesus, which, when I come to make decisions, inform my understanding and give me the 'right' answer. The Gospel is not about 'the meaning of things' for me, but about 'how to cope with things' as they are and as I have to meet them.

The Gospel is the imparting of an awareness of an ultimately good purpose in all life, and of a power within an individual to co-operate with that purpose, despite the apparent haphazardness of the world around him, and in spite of his own limitations.

The Gospel is that Jesus Christ is a new and living way for mankind to heal and be healed, forgive and be forgiven, reconcile and be reconciled; and that to find this way, consciously or unconsciously, is the purpose of existence.

These statements are, in my view, extremely significant, both for what they include and what they exclude. They come from a generation of deeply thoughtful and committed ministers, laymen and laywomen, mostly in their thirties. Plainly, if their position is to be described as 'radical', we must add some such word as 'Christocentric', for their radicalism and their faith are thoroughly Christ-centred, and derive from the things of Jesus, and not from contemporary humanism.

At the same time, they distinguish themselves equally

sharply from traditional statements of the Gospel. (1) They make no mention of the Old Testament before or the Church after Jesus Christ. They imply a Christ-centred view of existence which does not need any 'plan of salvation' view of history either before or after the Christ events, but which assumes that the Christ events have eternal, recurring validity. (2) They make no mention of the great texts of Paul, and their language, while obviously dependent on the whole New Testament witness, focuses either on modern thought forms or on references within the synoptic gospels. (3) They do not mention the fall of man, sin, atonement, justification by faith, heaven or hell.

I would be prepared to argue that this 'Christocentric radicalism' in fact does truly all that the old form of the Gospel did in a legalistic, literalistic and yet partial way. By speaking of 'healing', it implies a world less than what was intended by God; the old, legalistic form of this is the story of the fall, and the notion of sin and the devil as having 'control' on earth. By speaking of a holy and good purpose in the world and in human life, it implies the presence of God's will on earth, made possible by his hidden acceptance; the old, legalistic form of this is the classic theology of forgiveness, providence and grace. By speaking of the ultimate, the perfect, the end or purpose in existence, it implies the significance of men and things; the old, legalistic form of this is judgement, mercy and rejection, heaven and hell. By speaking of the relevance of the Jesus-mysteries to ordinary human life, it refers to discipleship as 'living in the absence of proof'; the old, legalistic form of which was faith and justification by grace. If you wish to put it so, the radical presses the old terms into existential meanings; or you may say that the radical takes what is given him in existence and in Christ, lives on the basis of them, and then finds, upon reflection, that of course the old orthodox or evangelical Christians, when they were truly 'ticking' and not just repeating slogans or texts, in fact lived by the same 'new and living way'.

So much for the relationship of this 'Christocentric radicalism' to the more traditional and evangelical positions. How, now, does it relate to liberalism? (1) It does not proceed from any rational argument about God or the universe, but solely from the person and work of Jesus. I happen to believe that this is a day in which all establishments, ecclesiastical and mental, have gone. One of the establishments to go is God. I believe that 'the God and Father of our Lord Jesus Christ' will only come into his own when the God of the philosophers, apologists and religionists, is seen to be dead. The radical says, 'Of course, no one knows anything about God. Only in Jesus is there a clue.' (2) It does not attempt to show that Jesus was a great teacher, prophet, or psychologist; rather, it insists upon seeing the angularity, peculiarity and unacceptability of Jesus on any rational view. Just as those looking for a Messiah had every reason to ask with John the Baptist, 'Are you really the one who is to come, or should we look for someone else?', so also modern man looking for his 'ideal man' will pass by the pale Galilean. Precisely. That is the cross, the *skandalon*. Only when you have 'got over' it, said 'And yet . . .', and started to live by it, is there anything in Jesus. Then you find there is everything. (3) It does not pass over into a vague universalism. It insists upon the absolute centrality of the mysteries of Jesus. It claims, indeed, that the evangelical and the traditionalist have not understood those mysteries. But it holds that those mysteries and they alone have the keys to life and death, and to whatever worlds there are and whatever God there is. (4) It does not end up in a modern version of the 'social gospel'. It seeks to discover the full meaning of the words and deeds of Jesus, but does not identify these with social progress or evolution.

3 Christocentric Radicalism

WHAT, then, does this 'Christocentric radicalism' look like, at least in outline? I set down my 'stand' in four assertions.

I. *I stand by Jesus Christ as uniquely God's Word to man.* That is, in more theological terms, I believe that all Christian thinking operates solely on the basis of the incarnation, and repudiates all attempts to set that unique Word within any context which might prejudge or alter it – whether that context be from the rest of scripture, or philosophy, or religion.

Let me expand and develop this in a number of ways:

1. To say that the starting-point of Christian thinking and thus of Christian theology needs to be asserted as in Christ alone is obviously to exclude in principle all theologies which begin from philosophical, ontological or scientific presuppositions and then attempt to fit Jesus Christ into them. My own feeling is that any assessment of the human situation *vis-à-vis* God in terms of 'ground of being' (as in Paul Tillich, John Robinson, or in more refined terms John Macquarrie) tends to load the Christian case prematurely and unnecessarily with a framework which is not native to it, and which might well prevent the distinctively Christian – that is, Christological – elements from emerging. If there is to be a 'system', it must *follow* a rediscovery of the meaning of Christ, not precede it. In this position, I would differ from Karl Barth in only three respects: first, I would insist that the Old Testament be seen alongside philosophical frameworks as not necessarily illuminative of the Christian core; second, I would insist that the creation of a 'system' must inevitably

follow the discovery of the Christological core, but be strictly determined by it; third I demand a *new* system!

2. To stand by Jesus Christ as God's unique Word to man is to claim from the outset that it is a full and adequate Word, meaningful and applicable to all men, all situations, all ages. If Christianity is mainly or merely a matter of personal salvation, then we must realize that our Word is *not* adequate to cover all men (most of whom are atheists, Mohammedans, Buddhists, etc.), all situations (most of which are political, sociological, economic, psychological – not religious or even 'personal'), or all ages (most of which never came within earshot of the Gospel). I believe it is adequate for precisely these men, these situations, these ages, because I believe that the understanding of Christianity in purely personal terms was a mistake from the beginning. Hence, I cannot agree with those (Th. van Leeuwen, Harvey Cox and others), who regard Christianity as an historical influence which has produced our modern secular culture, although I would insist that a secular culture is one in which we can get a better view of Christ than we can in a religious one. I would very much agree with Dietrich Bonhoeffer in his plea for a 'Christianity for man come of age', by which he simply meant that man is no longer in his adolescence, but can now stand on his own two feet, and that Christ is relevant for man in his moment of scientific and technological strength, in a far greater sense than he was ever relevant as a 'saviour' for man out of his psychological or personal weakness.

3. The uniqueness of God's Word in Jesus Christ makes possible a genuine and fruitful debate with those who take entirely different views of the world. If there is common ground with communists, atheists, Buddhists, etc., then it will derive from the Christological core of faith, and not from any 'lowest common denominator'.

II. *I stand by the words and deeds of Jesus in the gospels.* The gospels tell us, I believe, reliably all we need to know – notably, that the things that Jesus does now as the eternally anointed man of God are the same as the things he did here in the days of his flesh.

We cannot here go into the complexities of the debate about the synoptic gospels. But that debate seems to me to have issued in three lines which are now emerging, which augur well for a theology based on the traditions about Jesus. (1) The 'New Quest of the Historical Jesus' is based on a frank recognition that, since none of us was there, it is unlikely that we will unravel 'what actually happened' in minute detail. But we can unravel what the early Christians lived by, which they identified with what the early disciples of the earthly Jesus lived by – and that is more important, though only just appearing to be so. (2) From a number of the former disciples of Rudolf Bultmann, especially Ernst Fuchs, has come a new theological approach to the gospels, which sees the essential mutual dependability of the words and deeds of Jesus, one developing the other and illuminating the other. This is fruitful both as suggesting the reliability of both traditions, and also as indicating the total impact and significance of Jesus. (3) The study of Christology is, I believe, entering a new phase, in which whether or not Jesus thought of himself as Son of Man, or Messiah, or Servant, will take second place to a theological development of the things Jesus actually did. (4) Words like 'faith' which have previously been rather 'theological' are seen in a new way through the synoptic gospels, where 'faith' means simply 'preparedness for the Jesus-miracle to happen to me'.

The synoptic gospels have been the exclusive preserve of the liberals for too long! The radicals now find a new home there.

III. *I stand by the new Way of Jesus revealed in his words and deeds.* That is, I believe that the things which Jesus did here in the days of his flesh are the models, paradigms, and effective signs of a new Way for all humanity and all creation; and that those things are also for this world 'God's presence and his very self'.

I would set this down in seven propositions:

1. The calling of Jesus as man achieves and indicates the secularization of the holy, the realization of the ideal of the 'righteous', the localization of the universal, the temporalization of the eternal, so that now only the secularization, the realization, the localization and the temporalization in Jesus are to be heeded. This is the Gospel of 'incarnation', which cuts off all other roads to the holy, righteous, universal and eternal, in order to open them anew for all in Jesus.

2. The healings and exorcisms of Jesus achieve and indicate that God is not a God of providence, but ranges himself in Jesus against all that robs man of wholeness, and actively works for man's well-being. This is the Gospel of 'salvation' in so far as it brings relief to those who never 'believe' but merely allow the miracle to happen (*cf.* the debate about 'faith').

3. The preaching and parables of Jesus achieve and indicate the utter secularization of God and the Kingdom of God, and proclaim that the Kingdom is now *hidden* within apparently purely secular, selfish, political or mercenary actions. The Gospel of Jesus is that men deal with God through the secular, the selfish, the political, the mercenary; and that they do not deal with him or his Kingdom *directly*, but only through these things.

4. The meals of Jesus with outcasts and prostitutes achieve and indicate the forgiveness of God, present in the very deed of Jesus, which *is* forgiveness in 'acted parable', and is seen as such by the scribes and pharisees. The Gospel is that all men now stand before the feast of God's

presence. He eats now in Jesus with all men, who love or hate him, accept or reject him, hidden in the person of their neighbour.

5. The call to discipleship which Jesus addresses to some achieves and indicates the possibility of man's conscious and intentional involvement in and identification with the mysteries of Jesus, which in fact apply to all, but which are openly avowed only by the few. The Gospel is that man can be a fellow-worker through Jesus with God, if he will take up the cross and follow the way God's grace provides.

6. The sufferings and cross of Jesus achieve and indicate God's being at the mercy of his creatures. The Gospel is that God repudiates justice and power, and uses self-sacrifice to open up a new and living way whereby others may bring redemption through self-offering, that is, through Christ.

7. The resurrection of Jesus is the ultimate *imprimatur* upon Jesus. The Gospel is that this whole Way of Jesus is for ever accepted and significant before God, and thus the privilege and obligation of man to live by.

IV. *I stand by the Way of Jesus as a Living Way for the world*. All the mysteries of life and death are hid in Jesus Christ, which means that a new and living Way to significance has been opened up for this world in him. Those who are 'saved by his life' embody, proclaim and point to the deeds within the world which seem to be his.

1. This is essentially a mystique, a technique, a methodology, an expectation of the way things ultimately work, which the disciple is discipled to. It is, in the words of the last of the fourteen Gospel summaries (my own) a Way 'to heal and be healed, forgive and be forgiven, reconcile and be reconciled'. This continually throws the disciple back upon the seven-fold Way of his Master (Para. III), for the Master is the embodiment and the power of these secret ways of the Kingdom. At their best, the 'ethical'

teaching of the Epistles is concerned with the mysteries of this Christocentric existence, which is not first for the disciple's own sake, but first for the sake of Christ's world.

2. Salvation is thus 'the gift of significance'. It is the way whereby 'all things hold together in him' (Colossians 1:17). Salvation is at work, by Christ's deed, in the pragmatism of the world, in politics, in man's concern for poverty, inequality, hunger and injustice. But it is at work in all these not simply as some kind of 'providence', or 'historical process'. It is at work in them through Christ and by Christ's method and mystique of incarnation, healing, parable, identification, fellow-working, suffering and resurrection, the political and pragmatic forms of which may be in pragmatism rather than principle, in economic justice, in imagination, in sympathetic generosity, in self-identification, in self-sacrifice, in hope. Any particular event may not seem to be 'ripe' for the Christian 'solution', but that is only because we cannot see the inner dynamics at work in mankind now because of Jesus. When I am asked, 'Is there not little evidence for Christ at work in the world?' I can but answer in the words of a friend of mine (a Catholic nun), 'Is there any more evidence for Christ at work in the baptized?' In both cases, 'the eye of faith' is necessary.

3. The place of the Church now becomes clear. The Spirit 'takes of the things of Jesus and shows them to the disciples', as John has it, and 'explores all things' in the light of Christ, as Ephesians has it. The Church exists to rehearse in the company of those who believe in them the mysteries of Jesus – his words and deeds – so that the power within them may be manifest in the company of disciples when they set to work within the world. Their task in the world is to herald, build up, work with, and at times even precipitate, the mysteries and techniques of Jesus which have salvation for the world. I believe that this will mean a new, Radical Church, which sees its faith existing as

action, its liturgy and preaching as existing not for itself but for the world, its members (few they will be) committed to specific strategic vocations, its life geared to corporate and deeply considered action and witness. Such a Radical Church is, I believe, already coming to birth here and there out of the ruins of our rejected denominations, where a Church appears truly as 'the section of humanity within which Christ has really taken form' (Bonhoeffer).

* * *

The call of the radical to the Church today is, therefore, a call first of all to realism – to the realism of the gospels and to the realism of the Church's task today. It is a call to commitment – to commitment to Jesus Christ not simply as a factor in our own salvation, but as the new and living Way whereby we are involved in pioneering God's purposes for creation; and to commitment to the world which already hides the secular form of God, which is Jesus Christ. It is a call to faith – but faith not this time as persuading ourselves to believe in what is doubtful, but faith rather as being prepared to act on the basis of the utterly unprovable (that God stands behind Jesus). It is a call to discipleship – discipleship to Jesus, in a day in which all securities have gone, all proofs and arguments about God have disappeared, all kudos and privilege in the Church has been exposed.

I believe that this is a splendid and decisive moment in the history of the Church in which we have the privilege of standing 'in Christ'. The important things are not your beliefs but whether they enable you 'having done all, still to stand'. The important thing is not whether this opinion or doctrine is right, or that, but whether any of them can embody more fully the living Christ in our modern world. The radical seeks to open the door to every opinion, provided it is written in blood. Here, at any rate, already, a few of us stand. We can do no other.

Part II. Towards a Secular Christianity

4 After 'Christ and Methodism'

UNQUESTIONABLY, the most moving experience of my ministry has been to receive, over these last months, letters and comments from brother ministers about *Christ and Methodism.*

Typical was the word of a Chairman of a District. 'John, I hate you. I've had to throw away two-thirds of my sermons. But, confound you, I think you're right.' From a number of ministers in their middle and later years have come similar words. 'I'm afraid you are right. It's troubled me for a long time, all this experimental stuff. But I'm grateful that you have tried to show us the way out of it.' One well-known Superintendent wrote that he was glad to breathe again, as he had felt obliged to give up being a tutor for the Ministerial Training Department because he simply could not subscribe to the doctrines of Wesley any more.

So far, so bad. But, as an impatient layman from Carlisle wrote to the *Methodist Recorder*, 'what are we going to do now that the old doctrines have disappeared? Can we go on as before?'

First, get our bearings. It is significant that not a single scholarly refutal of the basic theological case against the doctrines has been forthcoming. In most cases, like that of the article of Thackray Eddy (*Methodist Magazine* May 1965) the case has been welcomed.

Right. Since theology formed our polity, discipline and ethos, they may well all be expected to change now that we agree that the theology is no more. The Local Preachers' Department will cease to require Wesley's Forty-Four Sermons as part of their examination. The Ministerial

Training Department, the District Synods, and the Circuit Local Preachers' meetings, will delete the questions about loyalty to 'our doctrines'. The Hymn Book revisers will scrutinize the Wesley hymns and the nineteenth-century ones, and will only allow to remain what can be sung by a contemporary congregation without hypocrisy or blasphemy. The Anglican-Methodist team will drop the dishonest claims made for Methodism in the Service of Reconciliation and in the Anglican-Methodist Report.

Of course, you could get out of this difficulty if you wished, by claiming that we didn't really mean what all the Methodist theologians have been saying in their books for the last hundred years. But that would hardly be honest to ourselves or to the other Churches.

No. It must go. All of it.

Is it then (as one enthusiastic Voice of Methodism man said to me) 'simply a call for a Minor Synod'? I doubt it, though that would at least mean that we were prepared to be taken seriously on our statements for all these years (and that would be no small gain). Actually, the much quoted *Deed of Union* is surprisingly useful on the subject:

> The Notes on the New Testament and the 44 Sermons are not intended to impose a system of formal or speculative theology on Methodist Preachers, but to set up standards of preaching and belief which should secure loyalty to the fundamental truths of the Gospel of Redemption and ensure the continued witness of the Church to the realities of the Christian experience of salvation. (*Recital 30*)

No, it's not a matter of heresy. Perhaps it may be one of 'finding Christ again'. I believe it is.

* * *

That leads on to the second point. Are we any nearer now to understanding 'the fundamental truths of the

Gospel' and 'the realities of the Christian experience of salvation'?

One point at which, on reflection, *Christ and Methodism* is admittedly deficient, is in its exclusive use of the term 'experience' in the special sense of Wesleyan experientialism. As numerous writers have pointed out, 'You must have experience before you can have anything else.'

I know what they mean and in one sense they are right. 'Experience' is simply 'life'. You cannot operate as a Christian at all unless there is some kind of basic underlying 'yea and amen' within your own soul. One of my friends is constantly saying, 'But you *have* assurance.' Again, I know what he means. You cannot be tied to the living words and deeds of Christ, however imperfectly, without some knowledge, sense, intuition, assurance that, at times, you are in the way in which creation intended you to be.

But there are dangers. On the one hand, we must never give the impression that we are only Christians because of 'what God has done for us personally'. God is God and Christ is Christ. He has already done all he needs to do (how blasphemous it so easily gets!) in the past and present ministry of Christ. Again, we do not make anything so when we 'believe' it. Disbelief is the human act. Belief is just preparedness for God's deed in Christ to be found in our mortal bodies, so that we live in him who is in fact life itself. A young man recently said to me, 'I couldn't go into the ministry unless God had given me an experience in my own soul.' I replied that the ministry could not be sustained on personal gratitude, but only on a life gripped by the whole of Christ's way and deeds. Perhaps the reason why so few young men, who feel the compulsion and attraction of Christ's Way get so far as offering for the ministry these days is simply that this old 'experience' bogey rises up before them. It began as glorious gospel. It has become crippling law.

Again, 'assurance', as we Methodists are supposed to believe it, is not so simple. One can speak of an interior sense of rightness and self-consistency and a flickering joy and self-confidence because at times one knows that the Way of Jesus has impinged even on our own way. But the 'doctrine of assurance' was of a special and distinctive revelation of the Spirit to our spirit, which one either had or had not, and which if one did not have, one travailed for. And that, for all but the very exceptional of us, is simply out, for a number of reasons that I need not repeat here.

So, 'experience' is a valid term if it means that we know only what we live by, and can live only by what we know. I say Yes to it, because it is 'life' I am talking about – our life, and Christ's life with and for and beside us. But No to 'experience' if it is going to be (as it is in our history) a waiting on God for 'special revelations'.

* * *

Third, then, what about the future?

I still think the first question is the theological one, the Christological one, 'What is Christ for man today?'; and then the practical one, 'What must we do to be in him?' We shall only become 'the bearers of new life for our age' (John Robinson) if we are attentive at this point.

The last chapter of *Christ and Methodism* on 'What is the Church?' has proved to be the most useful so far as study groups are concerned. But probably it is 'not nearly radical enough'. I can only write from my own stance, which is conscious and intended (I would not say willing!) service within the Church as it is now. But there are a thousand and one new things which we can all do now, even while our Ebenezers and our 'Blogg Streets' remain. And it is urgent that we do them.

Hence, I agree with Thomas J. Foinette that maps are

not making the journey, and the final guide is just a Call in the darkness 'into some impossible situations' (*Methodist Magazine*, September 1965). We must be prepared not only to move out from the base we now have, but also to allow and encourage the appearance of quite new Christ-responses, in quite new situations, in the world itself, in the places where the disciples of Jesus find themselves and are found by the needs of the world. At one end, we must persevere with our 'experiments' in ministry, worship, action and fellowship. At the other end, we must be prepared for a 'new form of Christ' to emerge from inside the world itself.

Basically, this is to ask, 'Is there a Secular Christ?' The basic question is still, I believe, 'Is not Christ essentially secular?', rather than 'Can we secularize an otherwise sacred and other worldly Jesus?' The proof of this, I admit, is yet to appear, and I have tried my hand at it in a longer book on the theology of the gospels, entitled *Secular Christ*.

The articles written on *Christ and Methodism*, however, suggest that it will not be easy to carve out breathing-space for a 'Christian radicalism' which is both derived from Christ and also thoroughly world-affirming. On the one hand, the conservative is likely to feel still that any emphasis upon Jesus is really just a return to the 'call to be like Jesus'. Thus David Calvert characterizes it:

> Vincent defines the Church as the 'human organization which seeks to extend the ministry of Christ in the world'. This ministry is that of the Lord Christ appealing to the man in us to become his disciples by our deeds for him: to live his life as far as we can. (*Methodist Magazine*, February 1966; *cf.* also *Preacher's Quarterly*, January 1966)

If it was just a question of 'only a call to be like Jesus', then, we must frankly admit, many outside the Church would say that it was time we heard it. In fact, however, Calvert quotes only one-half of what I wished to say about the Church. My very next sentence goes on: 'The Church is the organism which may become the living Body of Christ when it is doing the deeds of Christ' (p.90). I continue:

> The Church is not the Kingdom, but serves the Kingdom. It is not the Body of Christ, but exists to dramatize, minister and show forth the Body of Christ. It is not merely the human company of believers, because it is not constituted by human opinions or even groups, but only by the action of Christ which identifies itself with, or is hidden within, what the Church does.

Thus, when Calvert goes on to ask whether the Church as a do-gooding organization is really needed in the modern welfare state, he has missed the Christological point I am trying to make.

On the other hand (the conservatives having been, as I observed, mainly silent), there were others who found the first statement of the position 'considerably less radical than is necessary'. This is basically the complaint of Raymond Short (*Methodist Magazine*, March 1966), who seeks to answer 'deeper questions', beginning with 'the primary fact of relationship with God'. This is not dissimilar to the Bishop of Woolwich's response, when he seeks to begin, not with Christ, but with 'all that is genuinely human life'. John Robinson's article, 'Rocking the Radical Boat, Too' (*Prism*, March 1965) dubbed the book 'antihumanistic Christocentric fundamentalism'.

Can there be a theology which is at once Christocentric (as I claim all Christian theology must be) and also world-affirming? Can there be a theology which both accepts and rejoices in the new manhood in Christ, while at the same time not denying the depth and significance in all human life? Can Christ be both the Master of the essential little group of disciples, yet also the hidden Source of human wholeness? Can we find Christ or man today without beginning simultaneously with both? And what happens when Christ says one thing and modern man says another?

There is plenty of ground to cover yet!

5 Radicals in search of an Ethic

'REDEMPTION, Recreation and Renewal', the Convention was called. All the old slogans rained down like fire. 'Let us go in and fight the battle.' 'I fear I am preaching to the converted.' 'The great opportunities of our day and age.' 'If we don't beat this, it will beat us.' 'We need to harness our resources and stake out a new future for our children.' 'This is something that all of us can play his small part in.'

I felt at home – distressingly, but also comfortingly. Around me, reactions seemed to be the same. Three hundred of us departed to carry on the fight with renewed ——

Where were we? The Methodist Revival Fellowship? The opening jamboree of the Renewal Group Political Action Committee? CND, maybe, or a Vietnam Protest meeting? None of them. In a day when we flee in terror at words Christian, long, or difficult, 'Redemption, Recreation and Renewal' was the title of the Annual Convention of the North West Civic Trust on 17 June 1965. Myself, happily (I think) the only cleric present.

Sufficiently, the parable may say to us that in a day in which we are all being told to ask ourselves, 'should a truly contemporary person pray (or go to church, or imbibe soft drinks, or believe in God)?', there are people way outside the Church who do not take the world as it is and say, 'let's get matey with it'; but on the contrary go charging into it (with appropriate evangelical sensitivity) to set it right, or at least set it more to rights according to their own missionary vocation. Sufficiently, the parable may remind us that in a day in which we so much doubt the content or intelligibility of theological words that on most great questions we believe ourselves called to maintain a discreet, tolerant, unexceptionable silence, there are people outside the Church taking up our so-called empty concepts and discovering them afresh in secular situations.

There are two things – gospel and judgement, as ever, in them both. First, the theological meaning of the secular – whether there is a presence of Christ in 'contemporary secular political programmes'. Second, the possibility for Christian action – whether there is a 'deed in Christ' which the disciples must share. *New Directions*, summer 1965 condemned *Christ and Methodism* in one breath for claiming that Christ or Christianity could 'gain much from remaining parasitic on what might be called post-radical politics'; and in the next breath for being 'activist', in the sense of 'the political-Christian crusade'. The two elements are not contrary one to the other. But for discussion, they need to be seen separately. To be condemned for the one is not necessarily to be condemned for the other.

The first – the secular presence of Christ at the 'points of redemption' in modern life – is the line laid out in Colossians 1. 'All things hold together in him.' 'What has life has him.' The criteria are, as Harvey Cox puts it in his excellent and pioneering *The Secular City*, Christ's work as bringer of *kerygma*, *diakonia*, *koinonia* and 'exorcism'; or, as I have put it, Christ's work in incarnation, in healing, in self-identification, in suffering, and in rule. It is not a question of being 'parasitic' on modern secularization. Rather it is a question of asking how far the products of secularization are already the 'fruits of the Gospel', and in what areas and directions 'the things done in Christ' are being done in the contemporary secular world. This is controversially worked out by Harvey Cox. His interpretations may be questioned, but his Christological starting-point is vital and unassailable. If this element was not stressed in *Christ and Methodism*, it was only because I had written so much on it in other places. But it remains absolutely essential.

The point is worth stressing. What I have so far missed among 'radicals' is any preparedness to take the basic Christian theological – that is, Christological – categories seriously. Too often we are told to begin with some mythical paragon called 'a truly contemporary person', and then adjust our faith so that it can be indistinguishable from what he already is. Prayer, hymns, new testament, church, connexional oddities, ethical narrow-mindednesses and the rest have to be excluded simply because modern man finds them (we are told) irrelevant or curious. As a matter of fact, the kind of in-group ceremonials, prejudices and traditions which contemporary man is supposed to find amusing in the Church, he finds vastly meaningful in Rotary, Freemasons, golf club or working men's club. It is not, in fact, the rigmarole he finds ludicrous, but the Church which isn't remotely what it should be – the disciples of one Jesus Christ. He is not going to come back to us because we assure him we really don't do anything he doesn't do already. He is convinced of that now. He is only going to come back – or at least take a look at us – when we are producing the goods of Christian discipleship. Actually, I think this painful truth has dawned on the Anglican so-called radicals. *Prism*, which has flogged the old 'don't bother to be religious, just be secular' line, now hands over to *New Christian*, which at least in title promises to be greatly more useful. *New Directions*, if it is not careful, will be left out on the limb that *Prism* deftly abandoned.

Thus, the vital issue is not 'can we be Christian and secular?' In so far as we are any use at all today, we are already secular. The vital issue is, 'is there a secular Christ?', or 'is there a secular form of the Christian, or the Church?' And this does not mean, 'how little unlike everything else can we be?' but rather, 'what must *we* do to be in Him?' (*Christ and Methodism*, p.63). This is not a pious devotional exercise, but the real-life, ethical – existential, if that's what you mean by it – question answered by every man in his own time. Slavery, democracy, social reform, war, racialism, secularism – every one of them has been answered by Christians in their own time asking, 'What here must we do to be in him?' The fact that others might agree on the deed without the theology has never over-concerned a Church that at its best has believed that the Holy Spirit was not confined to its activities. The search for 'what we have distinctively to offer as Christians' is understandably crap to the non-Christian. It is only meaningful within a Christian dogmatic position. But it is quite essential there, so that the first conclusion must be that there is no escape from the theological question into the ethical, but rather that the ethical *is* the theological – or, for the Christian, the Christological. The world indeed 'writes the agenda' (it does so, whether we intend it to or not). Our task is to discover what we have to contribute to it.

The second element – the possibility of Christian action (or actions) – is obviously derivative from the first. Taking the five Christological categories mentioned earlier, one may describe the Christian perspectives as servanthood, healing, identification, suffering and rule (the latter I would identify with Harvey Cox's 'kerygmatic' perspective). Already within these perspectives, one may distinguish basically 'passive' from basically 'activistic' elements. Identification means sensitivity to each man, for one knows not in whom the Lord is present; suffering means willingness to accept rejection and pain as part of discipleship. The 'constructive value' of these operations has always been secondary to their Christ-dictated character. Contemporarily, 'pro-existence' corresponds to the first, 'non-violence' to the second. ('Pacifism' as still hawked by the older Peace Fellowship members is a problem either way.) Both pro-existence and non-violence are techniques which are understood by the Christian to 'work', because of what he sees in Christ. There is an 'activistic' element also, inasmuch as identification and suffering are not simply matters of 'attitude' or interior postures, but in fact can only become 'actual' in deeds.

The Church's actions in healing, servanthood and rule are more openly 'for the world'. Even here, however, the nature of Christ's work in these areas determines the expectations, methods and areas of concentration. If one has the love of Christ, he does the deeds of Christ. Without the deeds of Christ, the love of Christ is not present. The New Testament alternates in emphasis between both of these, and it is as fruitless to ask whether Christ was Christ by nature or Christ by deeds – modern Christology, for the record, favours the latter – as to ask whether we are saved (whatever that means . . .) by interior or exterior conformity to Christ. Thus, I would have thought – once more, *pace* the *New Directions* review – that *Christ and Methodism* was not a book of despair about the Church, but rather one of excessive optimism, as it holds out the real possibility of Christ-incorporation through life itself.

The relevance of all this to traditional Christian ethics is hardly difficult to find. The traditional understanding of the Christian was that he was a person who got 'saved', or converted, and joined the Church, and that in so doing he came to take on also the ethical positions of the Church he had joined. These varied greatly: conscientious objection to military service in the early Church, (though more from political aloofness than pacificism) or among the Mennonites; unwillingness to take part in or heed civil government in the case of some Reformation sects and early Baptists; abstention from money, sex and self-determination in the case of monasticism; abstention from gaming, swearing, whoring, backbiting and drunkenness in the case of the early Methodists; not drinking for the modern Anglo-Saxon Methodist, not smoking for the modern European Methodist. Now, some kind of in-group morality of do's and don'ts is completely unavoidable in any voluntary association of people. It is also unavoidable in the case of families. There is no particular value in slating our modern Methodist in-group morality. The absence of drink, gambling and extra-marital sex is no more to be ashamed of than their excessive presence in the kind of 'secular' society of modern middle-class success which we are supposed to put in its place. It would, in fact, be very interesting to know *why* some modern Methodists get so wild about their fathers' in-group behaviour. If it is simply that the university-trained, 'educated' Methodist sets up for himself a standard of success and fulfilment dictated by upper-middle-class contemporary society, then let him be assured that he cannot 'be like them' simply by imitating their behaviour, for their behaviour is dictated by a view of life which is avowedly non-Christian. Of course, he can get 'converted' their way, just as they can get converted his way. But you cannot pretend to be what you are not. Or if it is bishops at sherry parties that are the rub, then let us assure ourselves that, in my experience (having been at a few without losing my head), the kind of 'public image' of the Christian there presented is as completely irrelevant in society as the one of abstention we find so embarrassing. Let's face it that the Church has never been able to afford the luxury of secularist high life, wine-drinking with the influentials, and the rest, except in states where the Church has enjoyed some kind of establishment. The days of establishment are over. There is little point in our aping the by-products of the Anglican myth at a time when the Christians in the Church of England are anxious to make their Church Christian. The in-group moralities of the Church of England are understandably different from ours, owing to the kind of people they have had over the last two hundred years. The landed gentry simply did not go in for divorce, racial integration or popular religion.

If a brash campaign against the traditional prejudices will only end up in a face without a nose, this can but point up the exciting area left open for real progress. The abstentions were always the results of sociological and economic factors, with Scripture brought in as required. But you can't suddenly cease to 'belong', sociologically and economically. What you can do is cease to talk about absolutes, realize that we can't help being the people we are, and then set about seeing whether there are not areas in positive action in which we can perhaps find ourselves being formed anew by response to new situations. Within the Church, as within families, there will have to be a continuation of the 'things done and things not done'. To cease balanced and informed instruction on the facts about alcohol, gambling and extra-marital sex would be as stupid as we are at present in not giving, additionally, balanced and informed instruction on the facts about race, modern weapons, world poverty, drugs, crime and capital punishment. Within both sets, the teaching will be – as it is now, in any case, more and more becoming – 'situational', 'inductive'. But, of course, for the Christian, part of the situation is that Christ is in the midst of the problem; one of the facts from which you deduce your morality is that if there are no 'propositions', there is a 'presence'.

But the result of all this is not, as John Robinson claims in *Christian Morals Today*, 'starting from the primacy of persons and personal relationships', not 'Christianity as "humanism within a mystery" '. Rather it is a willingness for Christ to dictate the relationships, the humanism, the presence, the situation. There will not be 'moral instruction' in the old sense – I doubt if much survives now except in out-of-the-way Sunday schools – but there will be new relevance in our teaching about Christ, if it is to be vitally necessary to the discovery of our present secular discipleship. There has for a long time been a vast chasm between the 'stories about Jesus' and the 'moral instruction' sections in church and Sunday school curricula. The chasm must be bridged. 'Moral instruction' in the old sense will not survive. But 'moral instruction' in any sense whatsoever will not survive some of the present advocates of 'new morality' with their superficial comments on chastity and charity. 'New morality' is a highly secondary need to 'new discipleship'.

And new discipleship is going to emerge when we hold with equal openness and tenacity both to the modern secular world and to the contemporary Christ. The tragedy of the old ethic is not that it negated the world, but that it did not take the world seriously enough. Its weakness was not that it was world-renouncing, but that the renunciations – and some are necessary in any view of life, be it morality or discipleship – were seen as ends in themselves, and not as means whereby the world could be saved. The renunciations were inadequate because they were dictated by a selfish concern to keep the soul 'unspotted from the world'. There will still be renunciations when we ask for the deeds demanded by the deeds of Christ. But they will be merely disciplines that enable us to get on with the real job of showing the deeds of Christ. For they alone, for us or for the world, have the hope of wholeness, reconciliation, justice. What they are, and 'what we must do to be in him', are now the sixty-four thousand dollar questions.

6 Defining a new Radicalism

THE term 'radicalism' covers a multitude of positions, and creates strange bed-fellows. The contemporary Christian radicalism represented by many theologians is, I insist, neither specifically Christian nor particularly radical. That need not be repeated here.

My radicalism began with what I would call 'Donald Soper' radicalism. It is seventeen years since I first came under the spell of it – and of him. In many respects I stand with it still, and certainly in terms of friendship and affection for its exemplar I stand entirely with it. But it is now a different world. At 20, I attended my first Methodist Sacramental Fellowship Conference, began twelve years of yearly campaigning with the Order of Christian Witness, looked in on my first Methodist Peace Fellowship meeting, and decided to vote Labour, which I have done ever since. Now I have come to see that sacramentalism, evangelism, pacifism and socialism cannot any longer be our resting places as radicals. I have had to recognize that we – or at least I – have been led beyond them: building on them but going beyond them.

I do not regard this as a question, in any sense, of what is right and what is wrong, of what is new and of what is not so new. Radicalism of any kind is basically and simply a statement of positions. All I can do is to state why I take the positions I now take and relate them to Lord Soper's four positions.* This may be a useful way in which to indicate the relation of the views some of us

*As stated in a series of articles entitled 'Viewpoint', *Methodist Recorder*, March–April 1967

now hold to positions which are already fairly clearly delineated, known and respected among us.

Lord Soper's radicalism had advantages which are not likely to apply to our versions, not least because we live in a world in which the ideas against which it was contrasted are now different. Sacramentalism was needed as a corrective to crude experientialism; intelligent evangelism was needed to correct fundamentalistic conversion-mongering; pacifism to correct the idolatry of war; socialism to give an ideology to the pre-welfare state exploited masses.

But it is at least arguable that the debates have now shifted in each case.

'SACRAMENTALISM' OR 'MYSTERY'?

Let us take, first, eucharistic worship, or sacramentalism.

The debate today is not about sacraments or experience as ways of receiving Christ, but rather about the nature of the Christ and the Christianity which are to be received. In other words, the debate has shifted from an argument about the *how* to the *what*, from the *mode* to the *content*. Only when the 'what', the 'content' have been got right, or got right in a new way for our time, do we need to discuss again the 'how', the 'mode' of encountering them.

Most of us take for granted 'sacramental worship'. We do not need to stand any longer with the Methodist Sacramental Fellowship which, in my experience, sometimes seemed to be more concerned with the minutiae of the 1662 rite, or with being an Anglo-Catholic group within Methodism, than it did with bodying forth the realities of Christ in freedom and clarity in the company of his disciples. I have no interest in ensuring that I include 'the burden of them is intolerable', in the midst of Cranmer's Communion liturgy, when for me that whole liturgy has little or no chance of conveying the Christian mysteries, much less conveying them to modern man.

In place of sacramentalism as a 'debating point' or a stand-point, the radical today would bid for the total mystery of Christ. In place of 'concentrating their spiritual attentions upon the Cross', he concentrates on Christ's total work of healing, ministry, parables, self-identification, passion and resurrection. In place of the eucharistic offering as 'the means of grace and the core of fellowship', I would have to put (i) the meals of the earthly and the risen Jesus alongside the Last Supper meal, (ii) the true meals of modern disciples as they eat together, and (iii) the meals of Jesus then, and his disciples now, with the publicans and sinners.

In all this, I am far from denying the place of the Last Supper as commemoration or as re-enactment. I am only saying that for me it becomes life-giving and relevant (and thus converting) when it is seen not only as 'the look at the crucified' but also as 'the look at the living' Lord. We certainly want sacramental worship. But the sacramental worship some of us now seek is aimed at sacramentalizing the whole Christ, the 'Christ in all his offices' (Wesley), and not alone the crucified Saviour.

'EVANGELISM' OR 'COMMUNITY'?

I cannot but write of the Order of Christian Witness with enormous affection, as I owe it so much, and still turn out at its beck and call when asked. Lord Soper suggested two main reasons why the Order is significant: first, because it witnesses to the fact that 'evangelism' must be persuasive rather than authoritative; and second, because of the vitality and converting power of the Christian team, living and working together and inviting the 'outsider' into their fellowship. I heartily concur. My experience in OCW is exactly this.

Yet this logic leads me further. The most valuable pieces of 'witness', in my experience, on campaign or off, have not been entirely spoken witness. Sometimes it was (as with the Mormons) the simple fact of the campaigners giving time and money to be there at all. Sometimes it was our willingness to go out into the open air and speak (much more often than what we said).

Nearer home, the 'witness' which has affected others and raised their questions has been almost always deeds rather than words. Giving Christmas presents to Moslem Pakistani families ('they're not even Christians', people complained), running a play centre for the use of mothers shopping ('I wouldn't do this for 1s. an afternoon', one customer told a helper!), or a Youth Club ('Why do you bother with us?' asked one yobbo of a coffee bar helper), being generous to people ('they're only making a convenience of you', we are constantly told).

All of these are 'witnesses'. I would call them 'acted parables'. Few people hear our words, inside or outside the churches. But give them something to *see* and they'll be there, TV cameras and all.

The point about the Christian team in community has been confirmed many times over. But for me it has meant a longing to see in Methodism something akin to the Iona Community. We lost an enormous amount by not having such a movement. Possibly the day to start such operations is no longer with us. But in the Renewal Group we have always had a passionate minority who wanted this. Occasionally, the idea of a 'Methodist monastery' reappears. And lately I have met with groups concerned with 'a twentieth-century Christian style of life' who need this kind of community.

We must let the future create what forms it will. But there are some new moulds beginning to appear.

‘PACIFISM’ OR ‘DYNAMISM’?

Many in my generation take pacifism for granted – that is to say, we do not think that war can be an instrument of good or of God. In this, however, we are with the World Council of Churches as well as the pacifist groups. The reason why many of us, who might otherwise have done so, have not joined the Methodist Peace Fellowship is simply because we find the issue irrelevant as a matter of principle, and impertinent and impracticable as a statement of policy. When invited to join, I have consistently replied, ‘Change your subtitle (“an association of pacifists in the Methodist Church”) and I will join you immediately.’ In other words, many of those most active in the cause of *peace* are no longer prepared to be dubbed *pacifists*.

Most debates on pacifism, as I have discovered by bitter experience, are simply non-events. All the old pre-war arguments are repeated, along with the well-known illustrations. But if they are pressed, they insist that the relevance of pacifism is precisely its impossibility as a practical policy. Heads you lose, tails they win. Most of us, as a result, cease to debate pacifism and get on with peace-making. Actually most of the younger Methodist Peace Fellowship members do this.

Real confrontation, decision and action, in the areas of modern life which matter at the moment, occur where people open themselves to the real issues involved. For the Christian, one of the elements in every situation is the living Christ. The other element is the detail of the problem. What has to be decided about South Africa, Rhodesia, Vietnam and China, the Arms Race, World Hunger, World Population and any other issue, will be decided by Christians with this double sensitivity.

Pacifism was probably a correct response in the 1930s, and becomes a viable policy, possibly as non-violent resistance, in very special situations. But something beyond pacifism is needed to discern the signs of the times and discover how we ought to respond to them. This I would describe as 'dynamism' – the dynamics of the situation, plus the dynamics of Christ. The determinative factors for action are thus living realities, not principles. They are the world, and Christ. I find it enough. But I find it better to operate in freedom and openness, on the basis of these two positions only, of Christ and the world, rather than to be labelled with one particular partial and variable implication of the Christ events, such as the pacifist position implies. Indeed, I would even say that my voice is sometimes heard the more because of this absence of stand 'on principle'.

'SOCIALISM' OR 'RADICALISM'?

Most of the members of the Christian Socialist Movement are people with whom, on most issues, I find myself in common cause. Christian Socialism seems to me to be irrefutably an implication of parts of the New Testament. I would even go so far as to say that 'the political doctrines of common ownership, corporate planning, national responsibility, public welfare and public service are the contemporary socialist expression of the Christian commonwealth', at least for Western Europe in the 1960s.

But to say that 'Socialism is the political expression of the Kingdom of God on earth' seems to me to go too far. What will this look like in a hundred years? Will it not look as over-simple an assessment as Harvey Cox's that 'the secular city' is the economic expression of the Kingdom?

As yet, I admit, there is nothing to replace Socialism as an 'ism', to start campaigning for. But there are signs that there soon must be. Many voices inside and outside our three main political parties demand a different form for political radicalism. Certainly, the present Labour Government has had little need or room for 'socialism'.

Do we not now need some other form of political ideology under which to start rallying support – and policies?

I believe that this is an area full of possibility for Christians. At present, radicalism oscillates between the new left, the communists, the anarchists, and the 'radicals' in the three existing parties. The Labour Party, as the party of the lower-middle class and the industrial worker, has little chance of being the cradle of a new radicalism, as its dependence on a class is so clear – and at that, a class which will increasingly rise in status, power and wealth. If Labour were to lose the Trade Unions, of course, a new situation might emerge. But one could hardly wish that on them at the moment.

The political situation in Britain, in other words, is at present wide open. He who goes into it under any existing banner, be it 'socialist' or any other, probably excludes himself from some of the most significant debates, and excludes the possibility of involvement in the new alignments which will come.

In all this, Lord Soper's generation gains by the clarity of its positions. But the positions emerged to deal with particular historical events which are simply not the events of today. What we must ask is: what is demanded of us at *this* moment, by the emerging issues of *this* hour, out of obedience to the Christ of *this* generation?

To ask these questions is, for me, to concede willingly and wholeheatedly the brilliance, coherence and relevance of the older positions. But we cannot go on worshipping the past, even when the past has such outstanding exemplars. Each generation must find its own feet, and find its own radical forms of obedience.

Perhaps the greatest sin of Methodism since the war has been not to allow the new generations really to make their distinctive contributions. Instead, we have worn them down in treading a mill created generations ago, which we all agree must go, but which still has to be 'worked' by the younger men until it breaks them. This September, as four District Chairmen have independently complained to me, six of the most important and strategic pulpits of our Church will be filled by men in their sixties – some of them newly appointed! Is it any wonder that many of our best men now in their forties are in 'permissions to serve' jobs? They were never given the chance to lead. The men still in their thirties watch the game with more than casual interest! The men in their early twenties, of course, find me old hat and have their own revolutions to stage!

Part III. Towards a Radical Church

7 Will the World save us?*

ALL of us in the Church today are much concerned with domestic housekeeping. In particular, we have to keep our eyes on the Joneses next door, the other Churches. Unity is the logical end-product of this self-concern. How can we be reconciled one to another in faith, worship, membership, ministry and mission? How can we manifest the unity so often already there? I do not wish to speak against any of this. These are important matters. The rationalizing and reconciling between us must be done. But I want to suggest that if we think all this is going to save us in the modern world, we shall be disappointed.

I would like, initially, to make three comments about the present ecumenical mood. First, the basic assumption behind our ecumenizing. Too often, this is still, 'I'll have what you've got if you'll have what I've got': the *Jack Horner attitude*, whereby we 'pull out a plum . . . and say what a good boy am I'. Is it really true, historically or theologically, much less sociologically, that we all have 'great truths' or 'distinctive gifts', waiting to be extracted from the pit from which we were dug, and conferred upon each other? Are we not now at the stage where we must say, 'Love me for what I am, not for what I've got'? It would be such a deliverance for us poor, humble Methodists not to have to feel that we must give the Anglicans something in return for their being so generous with their episcopacy!

Second, this essentially anthropocentric and reactionary attitude of 'pulling out our plums' has not been overcome

*An address at the first British Faith and Order Conference, Nottingham, September 1964

by all the talk of '*Renewal*'. Renewal can mean merely polishing up the old machine so that it 'looks new' or is 'as good as new'. And to say that it is all the denominations together which are going to be 'renewed' is more horrifying than ever. God does 'new things', perhaps out of line with what has gone before, not always 'taking them over into something greater', but also rejecting them and throwing them out. Are we, in fact, merely securing the continuance of the morass of our current denominationalism by 'uniting' it, whereas the future is going to require radically different systems, expectations and responses? Can a Church for Britain now be at all a united 'Church in England' until the revolution of renewal has broken us all wide open all over again?

Third, *the world at present does not want us.* Any talk of 'mission' from the Church as it is (whether united or disunited – and they would both be the same, as we have said) to the world as it is would be criminal. What we now are is why the world does not want us, and merely to 'renew' or 'unite' is not going to make us more useful to the world. For fifty years, the world has increasingly rejected us. We are not suddenly going to be accepted just because we cut our losses, join forces, and be the friends the world has been laughing at us for years for not being.

Shall we learn from the world, then? Can the world save us, if we cannot save ourselves? I believe that this is the essential question for us all in these coming years. All that we do in putting our domestic house or houses in order will be judged by it. Christ is 'for' the world, 'has reconciled' the world. And we are the servants of Christ. What can the 'world' do to save the Church?

1. Above all, we must *adjust our faith* to the facts of Christian revelation. The question of the meaning of Christian faith is completely primary – and that means Christology, not theological speculation. What is Christ for man today? Is the Christ of the New Testament in any

genuine and balanced sense bodied forth, let alone contained, in the institution known as his 'Body'? If Christ is 'the Man for Others' rather than 'the Man for Us', then a long and painful theological revolution is only at its mild beginnings. A Conference on Faith and Order is tempted to get the 'Order' sorted out before the 'Faith' becomes clear. 'Christ for man today' is primary. Indeed, we may doubt whether we shall be given any new 'Order' for the Church until there are a few radical discoveries about the 'Faith' for our time.

2. Is this moment not perhaps *a time of darkness for the Church*? Are there not periods of the absence of God, of blind atheism? And do not such periods sometimes herald 'a new form of Christ appearing in the world'? Those who have lived with the assumptions of the ecumenical movement all their lives must beware of the temptation to fulfil in their old age that which already belongs to yesterday. At all events, we must not conclude unions, patchings-up and rationalizings which belong to a period of confident denominationalism, but which are essentially irrelevant to the present world. They may well be also irrelevant when the light of God's new day breaks through. But that new day can only come on the other side of the darkness of crucifixion; and we cannot be crucified while we are still boasting about our 'gifts' and 'what God has done for us'. Perhaps we have to begin by saying, not that we are all so rich that we can treat each other, but rather that we have all *lost* the Lord. Out of weakness, exhaustion, frustration and self-sacrifice we shall find each other's hands and be crucified and perhaps rise again with another 'Body' altogether.

3. Relatedly, do not *the 'facts of life' of Christianity in the world at large* in this century indicate already the task of the Protestant Churches? Spectacular progress in mission today is not being achieved by our Churches, but by the evangelical missions (especially those based on the

USA), and by the 'deviation' sects. I suggest that the task of the Churches in the Protestant tradition, as over against the sects on the one hand, and the Roman Catholics and Orthodox on the other, is to find a truly world-affirming faith. But this does not mean concocting a *laissez faire* co-existence with a passing Western culture (as Paul Tillich and John Robinson lead us to do, despite the enormous value of their work). It means discovering new and radical obedience wherein the Christian may enter through Western culture into the healing and suffering of God in the midst of the world. This is 'pro-existence' for the world's sake, as it is; but only after it is first 'pro-existence' for Christ's sake, Christ who is already present in the world. Certainly this is Christ in the 'depth' of humanity. But it is not just 'any depth', but the *revealed depth* in man, indicated by what Jesus 'began to do and teach'.

4. We must stop hedging about *the presence of Christ in the secular world*, and start allowing our 'faith' to lead us to actions of faith. We all wish to say that our faith is 'related' to the complex issues of modern politics, sociology and economics. But do we not now need to go on and say *in what ways* Christ and his way might already be present in them? The world demands that our good intentions and beneficent interest in these matters shall now lead us to put our cards on the table. And why should we fear to do so if we believe that God in Christ is already there?

5. We learn Christ *in places where we engage in action, in deeds*. Ecumenically, we know that we can live with each other when we work with each other. In the world we shall rediscover Christ as we are prepared to obey him in costly obedience for the world, which at least will mean a discipline economic (tithing, for a start) and vocational (compulsory, or at least normative periods of service in world mission). The life of Christ is genuine secular existence because Christ is secular.

Therefore, the call to us all in the post-Nottingham period, it seems to me, is not to imagine that we will have done anything at all when we have concluded our unions or our covenants, except lay a foundation upon which the real work may begin. Meantime, in order that we keep the two periods before us, we shall require an attitude of *openness*, this time not merely to each other but to the world; *a patience with experiment*, which will demand that new things be done, even if they upset our union schemes, as well as our denominational systems; and a blunt *insistence* that the Church of tomorrow which emerges will not simply take account of the things we all have been till now, but will be a wholly new creation, created for and by and in the world. The faith which will unite us tomorrow may not yet have emerged.

Perhaps Christ, the Church's Lord, speaks to us no more the word of Unity which he has spoken for fifty years. Perhaps the world is already the 'place' of his appearing, the 'word' he has to say. So that to listen to the world is to listen to him.

8 What shall we do with the Church?

THOSE of us to whom it is given (or who take it on themselves) to let off occasional squibs within the contemporary theological-ecumenical-ecclesiastical morass must necessarily appear either excessively pernickety or else downright perverse. Yet we are in the midst of a situation in which many of the received 'goals' of the Church's present preoccupation must themselves be radically questioned.

'Unity' is a good example. Those trained in the post-war theological mood have received as accepted truth the discovery of the 1930s – the time when their theological teachers were staking out their positions – that God's will was 'unity'. Nowadays, you do not have to argue for unity. Indeed, one occasionally feels a bit guilty if, when one has been speaking on the Church's task, a questioner complains that 'you didn't say anything about unity'. 'Unity' has come to be accepted as one of the great cure-alls of our day, which will renew us, recharge us and set us free for mission. 'Unity' has become a mythical state which is taken to judge all intermediate states. As they say, if we know where we are going, we can best discover how to get there.

This curiously over-realized eschatology is a product of the centralization and common 'backs-to-the-wallism' which is the ruling force in all our denominations. Perhaps we are in an age of rationalization, of sorting out, of clearing up. If this is all we mean by our unity – economic and social and perhaps evangelistic relevance – then well and good. But that is so obvious that it hardly needs talking about today. It has been obvious for fifty years.

What now needs saying is that it will simply be the death of the cause of Christ if we bring together the decrepit, dispirited, disbelieving rumps we now are, and think we shall get a new Church out of the union of them. I can think of nothing more horrifying than a 'Church for England' to which we all brought our 16th-, 17th- or 18th-century 'distinctive gifts', carefully preserved in our denominational hothouses. If there is anything in the coming secular Church which has to do with bishops, or fellowship, or congregational governments then heaven preserve us from all having to swallow the Anglican version of bishops, or the Methodist version of fellowship, or the Congregational version of government. We have preserved our distinctive inheritances so long that we have forgotten that sometimes things are better left to the history books.

Perhaps God has held back unity from us until we shall have created new forms for the Church and the Gospel in our day. Perhaps unity is held back because we are waiting for the Spirit to breathe over dry bones, and God is telling us that the winds of change are the winds of the Spirit, and they will sweep us off our feet – or into our graves – ere the day of the Lord needs a body such as a Church to contain Him.

For much concern with the unity of the Church begins from the assumption that the Church is God's chief preoccupation and pleasure. Yet in history, the *ecclesia* was simply the end-product of the determination of men to look to Jesus and live by Him – or the end-product of the Holy Spirit guiding the lives of the disciples. If there were groups of people saying, 'Let's be Christians', or 'What on earth could it mean if we tried to be Christians?', or 'Let's get together and do something about the old people, or the rates, or the Pakistanis, or the teenage delinquents', then there would be an *ecclesia*, a 'calling out', which doubtless would issue in an organization. But it would begin with people, with a common concern, with the Holy Spirit creating what he willed – and only at the end would there be questions about organization, and whether to own a piece of property, and whether to have full-time employees, and what constitution the meetings should follow. The Church today is in the situation of being lumbered by all this clobber which previous ages have created out of their real and existential needs.

Yet another thing needs to be said with equal force: the real and existential needs were Christian, Christ-dictated, Christocentric. They were needs which people voluntarily and passionately came to have because of their Christ-devotion.

It is hardly surprising that so many still think of the Church as something making demands upon you, which you get out of if you can. If you are not slick enough you'll get caught up in the web. This kind of Church, as a settled part of an older generation, making demands like parents, teachers or employers, is certainly dying and in many places is already dead. The institution has already crumbled and no one is interested in keeping it going. In the places where it still remains, a generation will see the end of it. We have passed the time for belly-aching about the Church in order to stop it being what we all don't want it to be.

The real question is whether in twenty years' time, there will be anyone in the Church, let alone whether there will be any leadership in the Church. The real question is, Can there be a community of people committed to Jesus Christ? The real question is whether there are going to be any prophetic deeds, any acted parables, any new embodiments of our understanding of Christianity. And so far there has been very little to show. It is, after all, our generation which has the privilege of being in a position to be prophetic in a situation in which everybody is now realizing that the old patterns have disintegrated and the old expectations were false.

Or, put in another way, this is a day when the Church has no other reason for existing except Jesus Christ. You could say this negatively. You could say that the crowds no longer come. You could say that the Church no longer stands for anything in the life of the country. And you can bemoan all these things. Or you could say just this same thing positively. You could say that the Church has just come through a long period, ever since Constantine, in which it has been in an artificial position of advantage. And now this is finished. Christianity as any kind of 'establishment' is at an end. All the systems which previously bolstered it – scientific, philosophical, political, social, ecclesiastical, national – have disappeared without trace in the modern secular, technological, pragmatic world. It is no longer of any advantage to anybody to be in the Christian Church. It is merely an added problem to the few who go. And most people get along very well without it.

And the Church is now coming into a situation in which all unnecessary pretensions are being cut away, where all positions of advantage have disappeared, and where the only reason left for the Church's existence is that it is a community of people looking to Jesus Christ. And here and there, in every congregation I have encountered in the last five years, there are people who greet the news first with hatred and fear, but then with incredulous relief and, lastly, with incredulous joy.

So we turn to the gospels and find that Jesus calls his twelve disciples, first 'that they might be with him', and second, 'that he might send them out to teach and to heal'. What does this mean for a group of people who come together and say that this understanding of existence that is hidden in Christ will be theirs? How can they hold each other in this? How can they build one another up in this?

This is, I believe, the only question with which you can begin. Only then can you go on to talk about the Christian Church.

The first thing, therefore, is that the Church might be 'with Christ'. I do not think this is primarily a devotional question. We probably are in an age in which devotion is much more difficult than it has been in many other ages. Western Christians as a whole are certainly the kind of people for whom the patterns of mystical devotion common to all religions are least suitable. Yet traditional ascetical disciplines have as little to offer to modern, technological man. From our own secular standpoint we must ask, 'Is the "being with him" primarily a matter of devotion in the old sense at all?' Modern man does not pray, at least in the way in which the classical patterns expect him to pray. Modern man does not worship, and those who go to worship do so for reasons other than those who arrange it expect. Modern man does not follow the traditional 'requirements of Church membership'.

In this situation there are only two possibilities: either you throw out the exercises altogether, and become a humanist; or else you throw out the exercises altogether, and ask whether in fact they were Christianly authentic in the first place. If you follow the first line, you leave the Church. If you follow the second line, you go to the Christological core of faith and start asking radical questions; and in order to find others to live with while the search goes on, you seek out or create a 'Radical Church' which is either a 'little *ecclesia*' within your local congregations, or else an existing Church of whatever denomination where people are trying to breathe the air you want to breathe. In that case, you need to ask all over again what prayer might be, what liturgy might be, what a twentieth-century style of life might be.

The radical who stays within the Church – albeit a small, selected one – knows that 'being with him' always leads to 'being sent out to teach and heal'. He knows that most of the sermons about 'coming' to Christ in his Church, and 'going' out from him into the world never lead to anything, partly because the devotion or fellowship or whatever is laid on 'inside' does not theologically or practically lead to action outside, partly because the 'going' has never been taken seriously enough to be likely to issue in anything but middle-class bourgeois decency.

Part of the trouble here is our whole conception of 'teaching and healing'. Historically, these functions have been confined to full-time operators known as 'ministers', and the essential identity of being 'in Christ' with being 'a minister' has been lost. Recent self-conscious efforts to establish a 'laity' separate from involvement-in-Christ's-work-which-is-ministry have not helped. We need to see 'teaching and healing' as the task of every Christian. We also need to train a vastly different set of operators from our present 'ministers', to perform full-time and part-time some of the present deeds of Christ, in his name, in both world and Church.

Again, any new form of 'Christian action' can only come from a new seriousness in taking simultaneously the Christological and the practical questions. Some of our buildings are still useful as a base for such action. Particularly, the Church in the metropolis needs to become a 'ground for meeting', where the Christian insights may be played out or rehearsed openly or incognito. Church buildings which neither serve this need nor can be adapted as hostels, youth centres, play centres or old folks' clubs should be sold – even in the suburbs. Removed from their 'home', Christians might begin asking, 'What shall we do?' Techniques of witness, infiltration, acted parable (not just 'involvement' – we are all already cluttered up with everything under the sun!) will emerge. The central church plant and the local house group will be needed to train each other in what to do and what to expect.

If any of this is right, it is hard to know what to do about the devout men producing unity reports, missionary structure papers, mission policy statements, much less Anglican–Methodist alliances. Probably, the radical should wish them well. At any rate, they ensure an area in which radicals are born of frustration. As Jerome said, 'I praise marriage because it gives me virgins.'

9 A Church for the Metropolis

In April 1966, Albert van den Heuvel, then of the Youth Department of the World Council of Churches, addressed a conference of deans and provosts of English cathedrals at Coventry Cathedral.* His first talk was called 'The Character of the Community Today', which he described as world-wide, revolutionary, mobile, differentiated. His second talk listed twelve 'Functions of a Cathedral in the Community Today'. A few are already performed by cathedrals here and there; most would be impossible for them to perform with their present restricted, antiquated buildings. Some of them are possible for central city plant such as 'central halls'. All of them should be obligatory for the central city base for the Church of the future which will replace both cathedral and central hall.

Van den Heuvel begins with two introductory provisos: First, the cathedral is not essential; it may be a good tool, it may be a bad tool, it can be corrupted, it can be relevant; in itself it is 'neutral'. Second, the cathedral is not 'central'. The *ecclesia* is not 'central', but 'a place where those who hold themselves responsible for the community meet', a place where those who seek the presence of God in the city take counsel, a place where we are open to the world, and do not go to it with 'deductions' from our theology. Both points are relevant to any town-centre church situation. Only Christ is essential, not any kind of Church. Only Christ in the world is central, not any operation for training people to see him there.

*Albert van den Heuvel, *Cathedrals as Places of Learning and Influence in the Community* (Coventry Cathedral 1966)

From here, we take van den Heuvel's list, and seek to illustrate it from one 'town centre stand', the Champness Hall, Rochdale. It might even provide a 'check list' for others.

1. A SIGN OF PRO-EXISTENCE

The Church exists 'for others'. It is not 'the stable of the elect, where people take refuge from this gruesome world'. It is not the place where the people come for their weekly dose of drugs.

Many a central church or hall has been just this. Many who came were the suburbanites who could not face Church involvement in their own area. Usually, they come no more now. Sunday evening television meets their needs without the fuss of transport and the exposure to personal demands in shrinking congregations where they can no longer 'put on a good show', and where the preacher no longer bleats the songs of Zion.

Yet the great buildings in which this was intended to take place can still sometimes be of use. Champness Hall is only forty years old, built too late for its 'central mission' task. What could be done with its hall seating 1,600, its lesser halls for 500, 200, 150 and all sizes downwards, not excluding twelve complete sets of toilets? Whatever else it was not, it was a place which meant something in the town, even if only that its offices were visited daily by dozens who wanted National Health Cards, or a visit to the town's specialists, or an insurance office; or else it was visited by crowds for the town's speech days, orchestral concerts and great town events. To most, it was not a church at all. Certainly, the Church had set up a 'sign of pro-existence', whether it intended it or not. It used to worry us that no one thought of it as a church. We have now come to see that this precisely gives us our opportunity. The only drawback is that the 'sign' is so massive, and looks so much a part of the 'establishment'.

The renewal theologians rightly say that the signs of the Church today must be humble, modest, unpretentious. But then they also tell us, rightly, that we must have 'style' and 'professional competence' and 'a good shop window'. At least we have the latter.

2. A SYMBOL OF DIVERSITY IN UNITY

A differentiated, pluriform society makes a uniform Church illegitimate. The Church must structure faith in divers forms where people are. In a central church, 'many things can go on at the same time without harming unity', says van den Heuvel.

So, at our Monday staff meeting each week, we sort out where simultaneously to house the Young Wives' Club, the Ladies' Guild, the Male Voice Choir, the Church in Industry group, and the Working Committee of the Ecumenical Centre (I quote the bill for the Monday prior to writing), while at the same time leaving the Youth Centre free for its own varied programme on the second floor, and fitting in a travel agency's film show in the lesser hall. Sometimes, Stainer's *Crucifixion* rehearsing in the main hall is vitiated by the electronic guitars from the youth club. Sometimes, as in every happy family, tempers fray. But we have room never to have to say No to any request. Four years ago, we published a brochure called *Ground for Meeting*, setting out our plans. At least, the diverse and curious contemporary forms of 'meeting' take place in one building, and the boundaries between old and young, educated and uneducated, can disappear by the simple method of confrontation in the coffee bar. Now that even the Youth Service, that most separated of all social spheres, has to become 'Youth and Community' Service, premises like these, which have only used parts of themselves for youth work, will be of even greater value. If our youth club premises are rarely used for things like Over Sixties Choir or Play Centre (afternoons, with voluntary staff, for all who care to use it) or Nurses Group or Twenties Group, this is only because the club itself proclaims diversity in unity with its groups for climbing, folk singing, table tennis, writing homework, drama, dress boutique, or mooching around, meeting within the same complex of rooms.

3. A PENTECOSTAL LABORATORY

The redemption of the Babylonian confusion of speech does not mean that we all now say the same thing, but rather that 'everybody here speaks as it were his own tongue'. The poetic, the scientific, each finds his own 'language'.

This is precisely what is impossible in the local churches. Only at the centre can there be enough room, enough freedom, enough coming and going between the committed, the semi-committed, the uncommitted and those also ecclesiastically committed elsewhere! Here too one can afford to experiment, without the whole congregation feeling that its future is tied up with this or that among the many experiments. I am not sure that the aim is to 'integrate' the various languages of commerce, art, science, education, public affairs, music, humanities, industry. First, they each need to find their feet and their tongue as part of the Christian community, but as parts left very much to themselves, without the criticism of being 'separatist'. All do not at present speak their own language in church, and each must now be given freedom, alongside those with whom nature, culture or age seems to set him, to speak in his own tongue the wonders of God's presence on earth. Then, at any rate, people 'outside' within these disciplines would hear something.

Where, if not in our 'town centre stands', can the Church today ever dare to experiment, to be a 'laboratory'? Only when separated from the financial and personnel drag of the places which ought to close or be closed, can the whole Church be free enough to dare to take risks. This means that the central place will rightly go on resisting attempts to burden it with a conventional 'circuit' of other churches. Many of the latter have no future, and it will not ultimately serve the good of the Kingdom to cripple the places to which we must look for leadership and the patterns for the future by siphoning off their energies in desperate attempts to maintain the *status quo* in places which, by God's mercy as well as man's defection, must simply die.

4. THE THEATRE OF BASIC DRAMA

'How the cathedral looks is how people will see the Church' is certainly true of the central hall. It means that décor, lighting, carpeting, heat, availability, openness, welcome, sensitivity, and 'style' all belong together. This does not necessarily mean a vast modernization scheme all done at once. Instead, we spent £15,000 over four years, modernizing as we adapted various parts of the building for new uses, every time with the maximum discussion and contribution from groups of people, professional and amateur, within the Church and outside. In the main hall, we eventually settled for a central carpeted and well-lit sanctuary, with modern furnishings, but not retaining in the end the controversial machine-embroidered Christ figure. We would like to exchange the tip-up seats for something better, and await a donor! To me it still seems incredible that large sums are spent on 'modernizing' without any kind of liturgical or theological study or discussion. You cannot create 'a theatre of basic drama' for this age by simply repeating the hall or church of even a generation ago, and just doing it in modern materials. Much good money has been wasted this way.

The drama of worship is rarely possible in a traditional

chancel church or a traditional platform hall. Something between the two, neither one thing nor the other, is needed. As for the liturgy itself, our experiments must be 'not for their own sake, but in order to get the drama across'. Folk groups, reading groups, tableaux, movement, dance all have their part to play, without creating new 'forms'. Set words are more of a problem. Two years after writing out our Family Communion Order in order to provide for a television service, we are still uncertain whether we have not lost something of the spontaneity of our original morning order, in which the congregation made simple and obvious responses, and the minister extemporized through the ministries of Christ to his disciples and the crowds (the shared bread and wine) and to the children (the laying-on of hands). We also have a periodic 'Worship Workshop', in which our team of ten excellent local preachers guide groups of the congregation in deciding their own form of words, prayers, readings, hymns and 'preachments'.

5. A TEMPLE OF DIALOGUE

Every silly get-together where people talk is not dialogue. It may be merely 'pooling of confusion'. What we need is 'Temples of Dialogue, where people are invited in their own right, with their own language, with their own concerns, and are given a free place to discuss'.

The 'Ground for Meeting' policy worked in the places already indicated, but dialogue on a more serious and sustained level has awaited the founding of the Ecumenical Centre. Born of a seminal conference on 'The Secular City' in September 1966, the Centre quickly grew a working committee of thirty who planned its programme, and a perilous but open-ended clergy group of twenty-five who mauled over its constitution. Thanks to an Anglican solicitor member, we now have the best ecumenical centre constitution in existence (we have studied all the others!).

All this was not the 'dialogue', but merely prepared for it. Groups sprang up within professional fields, and there are now regularly meeting monthly a Social Workers Group, a Christians in Industry Group, a Youth Workers Group, an Education Group, a Youth Group, a 'Christian Style of Life' Group, and a Theological Study Group. Commencing in September 1967, we shall have week-end and mid-week lecture series, as well as pastoral consultations for clergy. The Extra-Mural Department of Manchester University is assisting us, and for two years we now have a United Presbyterian 'frontier intern', a seminary graduate, as co-ordinating officer.

Which way the Centre will go is now anybody's guess. It is strong enough – particularly on the Roman Catholic side – to stand on its own feet, and engage in a 'dialogue' between specialists, both Christian and non-Christian, at a depth and a competence which no merely denominational enterprise could have achieved. It cannot claim to be 'popular' – perhaps the Churches in their normal life, like ourselves, can be 'all things to all men'. But the Centre can stake out claims in areas in which we at present do nothing or do what we do inadequately and unprofessionally. It is a worthy place for the 'second Church membership' which Mark Gibbs says that every modern Christian is entitled to.

6. A CENTRE OF CREATIVITY

One of our members has always thought that we ought to have an Arts Centre. I doubt if we shall manage it. But our Conference Room, our Lounge and senior Coffee Bar, and our new Chapel, all sited on the first floor alongside the offices of the Ecumenical Centre and the International Friendship Council, were designed by the local College of Art, and will house a varying exhibition of their work. These rooms, along with a general meeting room, form the last stage of the modernization, to be completed in spring 1968, to an architect member's plan.

7. AN ACADEMY FOR COMMITTED INFORMATION, AND

8. A CLINIC FOR PUBLIC EXORCISM

Van den Heuvel allies the two. 'Casting the devils out of modern society' is not easy, as Harvey Cox discovered. We attempt it, anyway, by sticking our noses into public affairs, taking up issues with people in authority, exposing or pioneering or writing up this or that in our monthly newspaper, *Today*. Whether we are 'an Academy for Committed Information' is for others to say. But we post our newspaper to nearly 200 all over the world, we often find ourselves landed with pioneering or pressing for things (such as the National Youth Task Force), and we find our Church Bookstall (generously run for us by Crux Press) frequently doing business.

9. AN INTERNATIONAL EXCHANGE

Nobody believes us when we call ourselves a universal Church, says van den Heuvel. Any Church can engage in exchange, which is the easiest way to transform attitudes. We have found ourselves on the European ecumenical tourist list, and have welcomed Americans, South Africans, Roumanians, and others. The community of six bed-sitters which we have (two of them large rooms with elastic walls!) means that we are able to welcome visitors into an already existing family, which currently consists of two couples and three single men, working variously in the team ministry or in the town. Additionally the warden and the deaconess have separate flats, also on the premises. We stretch our accommodation to take in week-end conferences for students or others, or simply to house groups coming to spend a few days with us.

Within the town itself, we have 2,500 Pakistanis, and several hundred Indians and other immigrant groups. In

December 1963, just after the assassination of President Kennedy, we opened our 'Kennedy Club', which provided a weekly meeting-point for people from many nations. More recently, the Club has moved out into the homes of immigrants, and its co-chairman has been appointed honorary secretary of the Rochdale Council for International Friendship, which has recently set up its headquarters in our new office suite on the first floor, with a full-time liaison officer.

10. A BROADCASTING STATION FOR THE VOICE OF THE POOR

In concern with immigrants, we certainly 'prepared public opinion for what is a necessary political step to take'. In other areas, we are content with helping along. The newly formed Council of Social Service is a sphere for our prodding. The Family Service Unit has its offices on our premises, jointly with the Diocesan Moral Welfare work, until they grow too large. Since January 1967 we have had a magnificent Community Service Volunteer, who, aided by CVS, the *Methodist Association of Youth Clubs* and a few other sources, has been pioneering and organizing community service among young people in the Ecumenical Centre and in MAYC clubs, as well as working in our own Club and organizing a yearly Christian Education Movement work camp.

11. A TOWER OF RECONCILIATION

We believe in the philosophy of unilateral initiative and vicarious propitiation, of 'holding two parties together, and probably being destroyed in the act of reconciliation'. To be a peacemaker is often a bloody business. We have seen it ecclesiastically, internationally, ecumenically, personally, pastorally: the 'baptism of fire'.

I refrain from being more specific!

12. A MOTEL FOR PILGRIMS

We're not an 'All things bright and beautiful' set-up. Our folk are bloody-minded northerners, not plaster saints. But as *The Observer* said, 'they may be mystified by it all, but they look pleased they came.' And folk come from all over the place for Saturday conferences or Sunday services (no big crowds, of course) and 'simply pass through and get what they call "an uplifting experience" and are sent back to the road, or to their work, or to their homes'.

Only a few need an overnight stop. One thing I'd love to do is to open a properly run steak bar, where we and they together could have a good meal. All we want is a dedicated young man or woman who has done his or her training, and is prepared to step off the promotion ladder for two or three years to get it going. . . .

13. THE HOUSE OF THE VICARIOUS FEASTS

'Festive congregations, who can transcend the dullness and dreariness of their existence by tremendous feasts' ought to be in our cathedral/central hall. You can get 500 in our Exhibition Hall, and we'd love to do it. It'll be easier when the other Churches in the area see that we are there to be made a convenience of! And there will be no collection! Meantime, we make do with housing the town's 'big do's'.

14. THE HUT OF THE SHEPHERD

All the Lord's people are ministers, and our 'hut' is not simply at the Hall, where people come and see us and tell us their troubles; it is also the place where a group runs a caring club for the lonely; it is every home in which our twenty house group leaders take a meeting or go and visit someone in need; it is the class where thirty folk (not all our own members) do a course in counselling. You won't get in and out of the place without several people speaking to you (it's all planned!). This caring does not 'pay'. It is not meant to pay. But, even with the usual deaths and removals, membership has crept from 200 to 235, and 127 people have thought it worth joining us, in four years, 1963–6: 59 from other Methodist churches, 21 from other denominations or countries, and 47 as new members. The new members are not mainly teenagers, either. They are people in their twenties, thirties, forties and fifties.

If it looks like a success story, then strike it all out. It isn't. It never can be. It's just one small attempt to live as the disciples of Christ in one place. In many areas we are not doing what we ought. For many people we cannot be or provide what they think they want. All we can do is what anyone can do – find a piece of ground worth standing on, and stand on it. And then, having done all, stand! For you do not stand alone – and, as Albert finished his talk, 'when we have done all these things, even then we are unprofitable servants'. Only Christ stands.

But we must stand with him.

10 The Dynamics of Christ in Devotion

'How does prayer fit into all this?' is a question asked of those who have been dubbed 'new' or 'radical' theologians. As Bonhoeffer devastatingly put it, 'What is the place of worship and prayer in an entire absence of religion?'[1]

The question can be asked in a negative way. That is, it can mean, 'I cannot see how you can continue to pray to a personal God through a personal Christ, if you believe what you do.' Uncertainty as to the nature of the Divine Being, faith as 'hanging on to Christ in the unjustifiable expectation that God stands behind him', Christian justification as the hidden acceptance of God in the midst of secular situations which prove to be Christ-situations, the Church as the 'people engaged in acted parables of the Kingdom' – all this may be right or wrong. But it can scarcely be said to be immediately fruitful for the devotional life.

Yet there is a positive way of raising the question. If there are new insights concerning Christ which are being revealed to our generation, then must it not be that the patterns of devotion, like the patterns of discipleship, can in the nature of the case only appear gradually and by painful experiment? But appear they must, and appear they will.

This, perhaps, can best be illustrated from our history. The early Christian Church did not seem to have much 'devotional' life in the sense that we know it today.[2] It had its cry, 'O Lord, come' (*maranatha,* 1 Cor. 16: 22), its prayers based on the Jewish Benedictions, its eucharistic recitals. Clearly, the gospels, especially John, were used for prayer and devotion.

The first impulse to Christian devotion was probably the faith that God stood behind Christ, and that a 'new and living way' had been opened up, giving access to the Father through the Son. This access to the Father is described in the New Testament as dependent very much on what we might call the total orientation of a man's existence. 'Through Jesus Christ our Lord' is not an appendage to be fixed on to any kind of prayer whatsoever. It is rather that to be said at the *beginning* of any prayer, as at the beginning of any deed. There is no distinction between prayer and deed because both are part of the Christ-life, both being offered to God 'through Jesus Christ'. This radical re-orientation in Christ is described as 'love' in the Epistles of John. It reappears implicitly in the discussion of faith and works in James. The emphasis on 'justification apart from the law' but 'through Christ' in Romans has the same purport. None of these is primarily a battle about whether a man sets his soul right by 'believing', or by 'doing', or by 'devotion'. They are primarily attempts to state the radically new as it is in Christ, over against first one and then another system that appears to deny the Christ-way as the sole access to reality, or that appears to become an end in itself, a principle, a system, separable from Christ.

This essentially Christocentric view of existence has not always found it easy to survive. Particularly in the West, 'through Jesus Christ' came to be far more a formula for Christianizing a basically foreign understanding of the God–Christ relationship, interpreted in forensic terms. Even the 'Christ of devotion' was mainly the Christ of the Cross. Western liturgy, Western mysticism, Luther and evangelical piety are all on a par in this essential respect. The monastic offices centred attention on various aspects of Christ's person – but they were all aspects of his suffering and death, interpreted vicariously.

A return to a full incarnational Christocentricity in

devotion must be awaited patiently. Running through much of the work of the nineteenth-century writers and hymnologists was a genuine devotion to the Jesus of the gospels – the Christ of the earthly ministry. Yet this strain, issuing naturally in the Social Gospel of the present century, only stressed the earthly Jesus by ignoring all but completely the risen and reigning Lord.[3]

How far has radical theology moved away from the classic devotional concentration on suffering and thus self-abnegation? Is the only answer to say with Bonhoeffer, 'Only a suffering God can help'? This time, to be sure, the suffering is not the suffering Christ of medieval devotion. But a Christ who is relevant to an imprisoned martyr is not necessarily the 'whole Christ'. There are points in modern church and personal life in which 'only a suffering God can help'. But there are also points at which 'only the healing Jesus of the gospels can help'. Until we can get over our suspicion of the gospels because the liberal social-gospellers misused them, we shall cut ourselves off from the vital source of Christian devotion: the total Christ of the gospels, whose office as Saviour and Redeemer is but the final parable of his offices as Healer, Teacher, Rabbi, Master, Righteous Man.

Therefore we wish to try to seek for methods of 'realizing' Christ's presence which will take their lines from the real Christ who has been revealed: the Christ of the deeds of mercy, the Christ of forgiveness, the Christ who calls men to discipleship and service, the Christ who hides himself within secular situations, the Christ who identifies himself with man.

PRAYER AS REST

In this century, Christian spirituality has constantly turned to the picture of Jesus ministering to the multitudes, then withdrawing to the mountain-top, and then returning to the multitudes (Mark 1: 32–39). This has led many to teach that we must 'first find God in the quietness of our own hearts' so that we can then serve him within the actions of the world. Retreat from the world had to come before involvement in the world.

There is obviously a deep truth about the human personality in this pattern of meditation and action, withdrawal and involvement, rest and activity, disengagement and engagement. All this can readily be seen and accepted. The debate is not about the essential rhythm of human behaviour. The debate is about *where God is* in it all.

> Take George MacLeod:
> What debilitates our prayer life, I suggest, is our presupposition that the pressures of life are on one side while God is on some other side: interested and concerned but on some other side. With this supposition, when evening comes with an ending to our pressures, we are apt to go eagerly to God – disconcertingly to find a vacuum. We seek to fill the vacuum with 'spiritual thoughts'. The more we try the more desperate does the situation become: till in effect we say that we are not really the praying type.[4]

Thus, what we need is an understanding of prayer as withdrawal, rest, relaxation, preparation, even joy, recreation, 'a change', 'a holiday', 'a break'. Prayer is exactly the renewal one man receives from walking in his garden, another from playing with his children, another from smoking his pipe, another from listening to music, another from climbing a mountain. Perhaps our great mistake has been that we have worked so hard at prayer – or at least felt that we ought to do so. Whereas prayer in the sense of rest really is no more than 'letting go', relaxation. Prayer is the point of completely minimal activity and effort. It is not meeting God. It is withdrawing from the immediacy of God hidden in the secular into the inner relaxations of our own personality.

Is this Christ-related? Perhaps it is not specifically, although it can be the necessary withdrawal from reality that will sustain the Christ-man in his life of discipleship. To secure the prayer of rest would at least mean that we arose refreshed, not debilitated and frustrated, from our points of withdrawal.

The Christian heritage has been remarkably deficient in the creation of techniques whereby this prayer of rest can be secured. Despite all the 'bankrupt corner' devotional books, Christianity has ministered but little to the fundamental rhythm of activity and rest. We must therefore turn with gratitude to the Eastern religions. The monastic routine of Western Christendom assumed that holiness and right doctrine were best instilled by repetition of an elaborate verbal kind. The Eastern religions – and the modern advertisers! – know that the deed which becomes involuntary is the one that most feeds the personality. The techniques of Yoga have a good deal to teach us here, I am bound to say. I quote from a recent book on the subject.

> Western civilization dearly needs some of the undoubted psychological benefits which follow Yogic practice. Of these, inner peace is perhaps the greatest wish. Having fought two wars, with a third on the horizon, we all share a great, instinctive longing for peace. We seek peace of mind and peace of spirit, such as the application of Yoga is said to bestow. This deep, abiding peace is elusive under modern living conditions. Even those who sneer at the ancient Yogis' preoccupation with affairs of the spirit will grant that peace is the one thing above all others which our tense, frustrated civilization craves. They may dismiss the Yogi as a poor, benighted fool; but his self-possession and happiness they must envy in their hearts.[5]

Well, we know what 'peace of mind' has led to, via

Norman Vincent Peale and his friends. What I wish to establish here is simply that there are bodily methods whereby 'rest' is given, and that 'devotion' or prayer, as it takes place in human beings, must take account of the techniques of the body.

To 'Christianize' these is a large task, and I would not claim to be able to spell it out. But the need, opportunity and reality of Christ suggest that there must be a way. For a start, one may recall the peculiarly profound words which the apocryphal Gospel of Thomas gives as words of Jesus:

> If they ask you, what is the sign of the Father in you, say, 'A movement and a rest'.

To live in Christ in the world is to be in movement, in 'the yoke'. And this is also in a sense to rest. But to pray is to pull back, tired, 'labouring', in order to 'rest on the promises', to relax upon the acceptance, to rejoice at the meaningfulness, to laugh at our blindness at it and to luxuriate in God's presence in it.

PRAYER AS RECOGNITION

Yet God is still 'hidden'. The modern, secular Christian has the devastating knowledge that in fact he cannot 'find' God in the old evangelical sense. In this situation he frequently becomes a crypto-fundamentalist in his prayer life, and goes on repeating attitudes to Bible, God and men that he knows he does not believe in. Yet there is another possibility: that God is so much 'given' and 'present' that to start talking about 'finding' God is immediately to go back away from the incarnation, into the Old Testament. 'Oh, that I knew where I might find him' (Job 23: 3) is the cry of the Old, not the New Testament. And the New Testament Gospel is not simply that the roles of searcher and sought are now reversed, so that God is now seeking men, not men seeking God. Rather, the New Testament Gospel is that God has found man, and stayed with him, and hidden himself within him. So that I now cannot find God for seeing man, or find man for seeing God.

The incarnation not only cuts off every 'religious' approach of man to God. It also cuts off every divine approach to man, save that which is 'in Christ'. This is not to exclude inspiration through other religions, or through non-Christian culture. Rather it is to say that the 'eternal' as well as the 'human' side of the God–man possibility have been confined to Christ. 'Through Christ', of course, to many modern people is a restrictive, exclusive, narrow term. In the New Testament it is the complete opposite. Thus to say, 'only through Christ', is to open the possibility that all religions or cultures come 'through Christ' simply because 'what belong to Christ' is in the gospels so wide a term both in the present (incarnation, healing, teaching, wholeness, acceptance, forgiveness, hidden significance of the secular, suffering, new life) and in the future (as God's acceptance is always hidden, and will be revealed only 'in the judgement' – as in the parables).

Christians go into the world to find their brother, not to find Christ. Helping our brother cannot be a means to our own salvation. It cannot be done for the ulterior motive that Christ might be in the brother. The Christian today needs to know his brother not as a hidden Christ, but in the authenticity of his being as atheist, humanist, agnostic. He needs to know how to treat his brother as a man, even as a man 'in his own right'. A brother minister, Thomas J. Foinette, has expressed it:

> Surely, I go into the world to find *my brother*. Christians believe they seek him, under the constraining love of Christ. And, in fact, for many, that will be the way they find God, in losing self, and see in their own concern the expression of Christ's love. But we cannot guarantee this to anyone, and ought not even to try.

Thus, we do not 'find God' in the world. Rather, we recognize the secular as God – or recognize what in the secular has been revealed by Christ as being his hidden presence. Thus, as Teilhard de Chardin found, 'Whatever happens is to be adored.' For, whatever happens is the cloak, the veil, the outward appearance, of the ultimately acceptable. If it is not so, we cannot know it at this moment. To adore is thus the 'safe' attitude – 'in case' God is in it.

Prayer is not, in this sense, essential. The presence of God is not in the secular merely when it is 'discovered'. Prayer is sufficiently the rehearsal of the Christ events in the imagination, so that the mind and spirit can be so attuned to the revelation of God in Christ. This is essential. Our 'recognition' of it is that which distinguishes the Christian from the non-Christian, the believer from the unbeliever.

Prayer is thus essentially a rejoicing, a privilege, an ecstatic recollection in peace of the deeds which are perhaps recognized afterwards as the place of God's appearing. The child's 'thank-you' prayers perhaps come nearest to it. Nearest of all is the prayer of the first 'initiate' into the mystery – the Lord himself:

> I thank thee, Father, Lord of heaven and earth, for hiding these things from the learned and wise, and revealing them to the simple. Yes, Father, such was thy choice. Everything is entrusted to me by my Father; and no one knows the Son but the Father, and no one knows the Father but the Son and those to whom the Son may choose to reveal him. (Matt. 11: 25–27)

'Knowing the Father' and 'knowing the Son' means recognizing the deeds of the Father and of the Son. To 'know God' is not an experience but a revelation, not an activity but a recognition, not a searching but a seeing. The revelation, recognition and seeing are contained in the

Christ of the gospels. The disciple waits, works and adores. Thus he has prayed.

The Christian understanding of existence is essentially a claim to some secret understanding of what happens to persons and to the world. We believe that this secret understanding is that which has been given to us in Christ, not least in the gospels, and above all (for me at any rate) in the parables. Obviously, however, this cannot normally be experienced existentially within the situations of life. It is God's mercy that secular deeds hide the incarnate Lord. It is God's mercy that he remains hidden. To pray is to withdraw and to reflect upon the part of the world which we ourselves have been involved in.

Recognition leads as quickly to confession as to thanksgiving. Perhaps Michele Quoist has offered the prayers of our generation in this sense of recognizing the hiddenness of God in humanity:

> That face, Lord, has haunted me all evening.
> It is a living reproach,
> A prolonged cry that reaches me in my quietude.
> That face is young, Lord, yet men's sins have struck it;
> He was defenceless and exposed to their blows.
> Lord, forgive me for that face which has condemned me,
> Lord, thank you for that face which has awakened me.[6]

Or one may recall John Robinson's famous expression of it:

> My own experience is that I am really praying for people, agonizing with God for them, precisely *as* I meet them and really give my soul to them. It is then if ever, in this incarnational relationship, that deep speaks to deep and the Spirit of God is able to take up our inarticulate groans and turn them into prayer. It is *afterwards* that I find one needs to withdraw – as it were, to clarify on tablets and bring to obedience the revelation given on the mount.[7]

PRAYER AS REHEARSAL

Prayer is the return in the imagination to that which is ultimately valid. It is the memorial in imagination to the manner of our redemption. It is thus also the rehearsal before the mind's eye of that which is to be fed into the personality for guidance, judgement and release, from the saving realities which are Christ.

Thus, a man prays by turning in himself (*metanoia*, repentance) to his model and redemption (Christ) and to his world (mission). He sees each one in the light of the other.

The man who prays thus turns to the gospel narratives and rehearses over and over again the incarnation, teaching, ministry, healing, forgiveness, self-identification, cross, resurrection, ascension and perpetual reign of Jesus Christ. The man who prays is simply the man who looks to Jesus, who sees him as 'the proper man', who sees him 'working', living life to the full, rejoicing in his humanity, suffering alongside humanity, and doing this now, hiddenly, but still 'in this world'. In the midst of a good deal which I find neither intelligible nor clearly Christian, Ronald Gregor Smith, in a tentative epilogue labelled 'Prayer', has these utterly profound words:

> Prayer, therefore, is to be understood as the anticipation in the whole of our existence of that one End which is the reality of God. This does not mean that our recourse to the Spirit is the same thing as a spiritualizing of life. On the contrary, it means the presence in absence of the Spirit.
>
> So prayer is not an attitude or a formula, it is not a content and not even a form. But it is the engagement of the whole life in the hope of the End of Christ. It is in the paradoxical union of the choice or the decision with the givenness of the End in Christ, of Christ as the Last Man, the foretaste and the promise, that prayer arises.[8]

All that one would add is that the End can be over-emphasized. It was the *Beginning* in the Gospel which started it all. It is the beginning as recorded in the gospels that is still the 'feed-in' for it all.

The things which Christians do together find their justification here. The whole Church finds its sufficient *raison d'être* in the words and deeds of Jesus. The words of Jesus form the substance of the spoken functions of the *ekklesia*: in fellowship, in discussion, in preaching. The deeds of Jesus form the substance of the acted functions of the *ekklesia*: in worship, in sacrament, in witness, in service.

In this connection, the private rehearsal of the words and deeds of Jesus is necessarily more fragmentary and incomplete than the commitment to them by the company of Christ's followers together. Private prayer is merely the personal 'taking to oneself' of that which constitutes the 'body of Christ' on earth.

Again, if personal prayer is not the *essential* side of the human 'laying hold' on Christ (which the Church, in its proper form, is), also we must say that personal prayer is not the *essential* side of that non-human, transcendental 'laying hold' on Christ which the world is. Prayer is the ante-chamber. The Holy of Holies is the world. Prayer is the place where we *rehearse* the facts which are being acted out in the world. Prayer is the 'wings' in which one checks over one's lines, adjusts one's costume, before one steps out in front of the footlights.

The 'lines', the 'part we are playing', as well as the hero, the leading man, whose cue we have to await, is Christ. He is the Actor, the Actor of our salvation and the world's. We are his understudies one moment, his co-actors the next. The Church is the people who 'stay awake' with Christ (Mark 14: 38), who constitute the spectacle (*theatron*, 1 Cor. 4: 9) for all to see, the 'act' which points to and even continues God's acts in Christ.

Is this 'rehearsal' prayer? Or are we simply coming under Lesslie Newbigin's condemnation of the secularizers: that we rob people of 'the assurance of the transcendent', and that we ignore that 'prayer was a profound reality for Jesus'.[9] I wonder. It is at least arguable that Jesus used his times of withdrawal merely as preparation or rehearsal before 'the thing itself' – obedience in the specific, the secular.[10] It is also arguable that no one generation can see the whole Christ. And that perhaps for ours, the darkness of 'the transcendent' is being concentrated in the secular, so that at least we may learn one lesson.

Lord, my words are many and my silences are few;
you alone can judge the results,
you alone can see into their future;
Help me to see that this is as it should be,
And concentrate my powers on the task to hand.[11]

NOTES TO CHAPTER 10

1. Bonhoeffer, *Letters and Papers from Prison* (SCM Press 1967), p.123.
2. *cf.* Adalbert Hamman, *Early Christian Prayers* (Longmans 1961), and his volumes: *La Prière*, I: New Testament; II: Early Church (Paris: Desclée 1959, 1963)
3. Horton Davies, 'The Expression of the Social Gospel in Worship', *Studia Liturgica* II (1963), 3, pp.174-92.
4. George F. MacLeod, *Only One Way Left* (Iona Community 1956), p.160.
5. Desmond Dunne, *Yoga for Everyone* (New English Library Ltd. 1963), p.17.
6. Michele Quoist, *Prayers of Life* (Gill and Son 1963), pp.55, 58.
7. J. A. T. Robinson, *Honest to God* (SCM Paperbacks 1963), p.99.
8. Ronald Gregor Smith, *Secular Christianity* (Collins 1966), p.208.
9. Lesslie Newbigin, *Honest Religion for Secular Man* (SCM Press 1966), p.149.
10. *Secular Christ*, (Lutterworth Press 1968).
11. Peter Hutchinson, 'The Lord and My Neighbour: Prayers for Today', *New Christian*, 13 January 1966, p.15.

Bibliographical Note

Part I. Some parts of 'Here I Stand' appeared in the *British Weekly*, August 1967; *cf.* also *New Christian*, 23 March 1967. The last two chapters appear in 'Christocentric Radicalism', *The Christian Century*, December 1967.

Part II. 'After *Christ and Methodism*' first appeared in shorter form in the *Methodist Magazine*, January 1966; 'Radicals in Search of an Ethic' in *New Directions*, Autumn 1965; and 'Defining a New Radicalism' in the *Methodist Recorder*, May 1967.

Part III. 'Will the World Save Us?' has not appeared in print before (though *cf. Unity Begins at Home*, p.37). 'What Shall We Do with the Church?' appeared in *New Directions* Summer 1967; and a shortened version of 'A Church for the Metropolis' in *Report 112*, the 1967 Report of the Methodist Home Missions Department. 'The Dynamics of Christ in Devotion' first appeared in shorter form in *The Livingstonian*, published by Rhodes University, 1966.

For Further Reading

PART I

1. RUMBLINGS OF A NEW REFORMATION

J. A. T. Robinson: *The New Reformation?* (SCM Press 1965)
Gordon Rupp: *The Old Reformation and the New* (Epworth Press 1967)
Thomas Ogletree: *The Death of God Controversy* (SCM Press 1966)

2. THE SEARCH FOR A CONTEMPORARY GOSPEL

J. A. T. Robinson: *Honest to God* (SCM Press 1963)
John J. Vincent: *Christ and Methodism* (Epworth Press 1965)
William Hamilton: *The New Essence of Christianity* (Darton, Longman) and Todd 1966)
Colin Williams: *Faith in a Secular Age* (Fontana Books 1966)
Geoffrey Ainger: *Jesus our Contemporary* (SCM Press 1967)

3. CHRISTOCENTRIC RADICALISM

John J. Vincent: *Secular Christ* (Lutterworth Press 1968), 'New Bottles or New Wine?', *London Quarterly and Holborn Review*, October 1964

PART II

4. AFTER CHRIST AND METHODISM

John J. Vincent: *Christ and Methodism: What Now?* (Discussion Paper) (Epworth Press 1966)
Ivor H. Jones: 'Radical Theology', in *The Preacher's Handbook*, Vol 10 (Epworth Press 1967)

5. RADICALS IN SEARCH OF AN ETHIC

Harvey Cox: *The Secular City* (SCM Press 1965)
J. A. T. Robinson: *Christian Morals Today* (SCM Press 1964)
Sex and Morality, British Council of Churches Report (SCM Press 1966

6. DEFINING A NEW RADICALISM

Donald O. Soper: *All His Grace* (Epworth Press 1957); *The Advocacy of the Gospel* (Hodder and Stoughton 1961); *Tower Hill, 12.30* (Epworth Press 1963)
John J. Vincent: 'The Way Ahead: Between Protest and Politics', in *Peace on Earth: The Way Ahead* (Sheed and Ward 1966)

PART III

7. WILL THE WORLD SAVE US?

Rupert E. Davies and David L. Edwards: *Unity Begins at Home* (Report of Nottingham Conference) (SCM Press 1965)

8. WHAT SHALL WE DO WITH THE CHURCH?

Albert H. van den Heuvel: *The Humiliation of the Church* (SCM Press 1967)

Beware of the Church, Essays by Members of the Renewal Group (Epworth Press, to be published in 1968)

9. A CHURCH FOR THE METROPOLIS

Albert H. van den Heuvel: *Cathedrals as Places of Learning and Influence in the Community* (Coventry Cathedral 1966)

Gibson Winter: *The New Creation as Metropolis* (Macmillan Company, New York 1963)

J. C. Hoekendijk: *The Church Inside Out* (SCM Press 1967)

Colin W. Williams: *What in the World?* (Epworth Press 1965)

10. THE DYNAMICS OF CHRIST IN DEVOTION

J. A. T. Robinson: 'Pop Prayer', in *But That I Can't Believe* (Fontana Books 1967)

Malcolm Boyd: *Are You Running With Me, Jesus?* (Heinemann and SCM Press 1967)

Michele Quoist: *Prayers of Life* (Gill and Son, Dublin 1963)